The Bad Driver's Handbook

Hundreds of Simple Maneuvers to Frustrate, Annoy, and Endanger Those Around You

The Book the DMV Doesn't Want You to Read!

Zack Arnstein and Larry Arnstein

Illustrations by Bryan Duddles

Copyright ©2005 by Zack Arnstein and Larry Arnstein

All rights reserved. This book may not be reproduced in whole or in part or in any form or format without written permission of the publisher.

S A N T A
M O N I C A
P R E S S

Published by:
Santa Monica Press LLC
P.O. Box 1076
Santa Monica, CA 90406-1076
1-800-784-9553
www.santamonicapress.com
books@santamonicapress.com

Printed in the United States

Santa Monica Press books are available at special quantity discounts when pur-chased in bulk by corporations, organizations, or groups. Please call our Special Sales department at 1-800-784-9553.

ISBN 1-59580-004-2

Library of Congress Cataloging-in-Publication Data

Arnstein, Zack, 1980–
    The bad driver's handbook : hundreds of simple maneuvers to frustrate, annoy, and endanger those around you / by Zack Arnstein and Larry Arnstein.
        p. cm.
    ISBN 1-59580-004-2
    1. Automobile driving—Humor. I. Arnstein, Larry, 1945- II. Title.
    PN6231.A8A76 2005
    818'.602—dc22

                                                                                2005009676

Cover and interior design by Lynda "Cool Dog" Jakovich
Back cover photo by Jeff Rothenberg

Contents

SECTION ONE

Building Blocks of Bad Driving

You Are a Bad Driver

Quick Quiz

What does this sign mean to you?

A. Reduce speed, check carefully for cross traffic.

B. Apply pressure to brake pedal, look both ways.

C. Roll through this intersection at a safe and cautious velocity.

If you chose A), B), or C), the good news is you are a healthy, normal, patriotic American. The bad news is that officially, you are a Bad Driver. At least according to the unrealistic standards presented in that work of fiction, *The DMV Driver's Handbook*.

If you read *The DMV Driver's Handbook,* you will hear about an imaginary being known as a "good" driver who stops at stop signs, drives within the posted speed limits, always yields to pedestrians, and who, in any real-world situation, would be a *menace* to actual safety. This "good" driver is so hazardous because nobody expects this peculiar driving behavior. "Good" driving *surprises* real drivers, thus causing dangerous and costly accidents. For example, the following diagram illustrates the all-too-familiar results of a "good" driver making an unexpected *full stop* at a stop sign.

Where does this "good" driver pick up these bad habits which can be so dangerous to good old regular "bad" drivers? *The DMV Driver's Handbook,* where you will find guidelines which range from the merely *misleading,* like:

"You must always travel within the posted speed limit."

which fails to account for the universally accepted concept of "the flow of traffic" and ignores necessary situational adjustments based on how much of a hurry you happen to be in, to the downright *false,* like:

"A yellow light means you should SLOW DOWN so as not to enter the intersection when the light turns red."

(Everybody knows a yellow light means you should SPEED UP to BEAT THE LIGHT.)

While the majority of the information is false, some of it is well-intentioned but grossly outdated. We must revisit the suggestions presented in *The DMV Driver's Handbook*, keeping in mind that when our Founding Fathers wrote this historic document, cars were drawn mostly by horses and dogs. Thus, whatever rules may have been appropriate then must be adapted to our modern world.

Police officers sometimes fall victim to a rigid, "strict constructionist" interpretation of the vehicle code. But in truth it is a *living document*, and it's your responsibility as a driver to reinterpret the code according to ever-changing conditions.

The Vast DMV Conspiracy

If you've ever had any problems with the DMV, it is quite likely because the DMV is tangled up with a *large government conspiracy* involving not only the CIA, the FBI, the KGB, and the NBA, but quite possibly the Department of Agriculture. What is the purpose of this global, interlocking network of conspirators? We can only guess. But it's something, and you, the people, should certainly be aware of it. As Patrick Henry once bravely said, and this is a direct paraphrase, "We must fight to dismantle systems of oppression created by distant and tyrannical monarchies, *and the DMV*." [1] [2] [3]

---

[1] italics added.

[2] OK, the whole DMV part was also added.

[3] OK, the whole quote is bogus, but he probably said something like that.

In order to conceal the tremendous reach of their organization, the DMVs in some states are known by various aliases. Similarly, *The Driver's Handbook* is also known as *The Driver's Manual,* and there are differences in driving laws between the states, but these are mainly to confuse interstate drivers, like suddenly reducing the speed limit when you cross state lines on the same stretch of road, which is known as *a speed trap.*

So the DMV is a divisive, subversive organization infiltrated by French socialists—not news to anyone. But can they alone account for all the misinformation about what good and bad driving really is?

Another reason why bad drivers are so misunderstood is that they are unfairly represented by the *Good Driver Elite Media,* which constantly gravitates towards the sensational: the accidents, the car chases, while successful bad driving is systematically suppressed. If a bad driver makes an amazing left turn from the far right lane across an eight lane highway, that is not considered "newsworthy." By only showing the negative side of bad driving, the Good Driver Elite Media advances its pro-DMV agenda, and the first casualty is the truth.

So where can you turn for guidance? Until now there has been nowhere to turn. No accurate compilation of the values real, modern American drivers hold dear. Too long have our stories gone untold, our prophets fined and imprisoned, our ideals crushed. But the same spirit of fierce independence which inspired our Founding Fathers to drive on the opposite side of the road as our former British rulers still beats in the breast of every true American today. We still make up our own minds about such fundamental freedoms as which traffic laws are relevant to our personal driving needs.

Therefore, with safety uppermost in mind, in order to avoid the many accidents which result from an indiscriminate adherence to *The DMV Driver's Handbook,* and with Liberty and Justice for all, we present the first comprehensive guide to the rules of the road and proper driving techniques for you, the real, thus, "bad," thus actually "good" driver.

Summary

If someone got you this book, you may want to reconsider the cordial nature of your relationship with that person in favor of a more hostile, bitter, long-term grudge kind of thing.

CHAPTER 1

Turn Signals—Why Give Up the Element of Surprise?

We're all familiar with the monumentally boring regular right- and left-hand turns. However, *The DMV Driver's Handbook* curiously fails to mention a wide array of turns which are available and at your disposal, in an attempt to limit you to the few types of turns *they* want you to make. This is just one of the ways they attempt to reduce human agency and stifle our creativity.

We have recovered some of these omitted turns, and presented them below:

"The Quick-Draw Left"

This turn, essential to any comprehensive repertoire, capitalizes on the slow reaction time of the average driver waiting at a red light, by accelerating *without hesitation* when

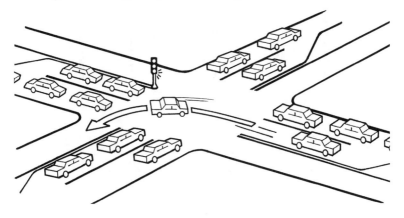

the light changes, crossing left in front of oncoming traffic, potentially saving minutes of otherwise wasted time, and contributing to the increased efficiency of traffic flow.

"The Jerk-Merge Left" (in some states referred to as "The Because-I-Can Left")

Especially useful during rush hour when the Left Hand Turn Lane is clogged with law-abiding, weak-minded drones in the Army of the Dull. In this turn you use your ingenuity to create an unmarked, supplemental VIP turn lane *just for you.*

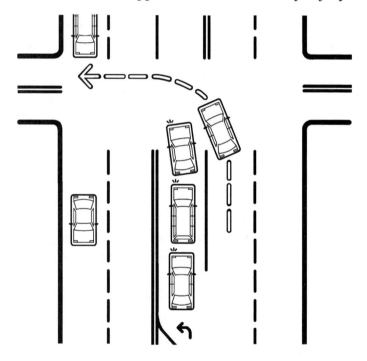

"The Gas Station Right"

Another turn designed both to speed your personal progress through a congested intersection and help relieve pressure from a traffic bottleneck. This scholarly maneuver is based on Euclidean geometrical principles. (Traveling along the hypotenuse "c" as opposed to sides "a" and "b" also reduces poisonous emissions and preserves precious resources.)

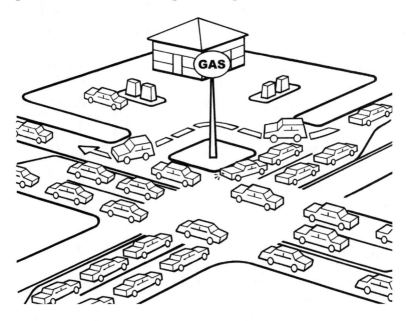

"The Surprise Left"

Turner gives as little indication as possible of his intention to turn left, certainly no signaling of any kind, slams on his brakes and waits patiently for a good time to turn. This turn has no redeeming social value but provides a certain unique satisfaction when executed properly. Especially effective immediately after accelerating to cut in front of another car.

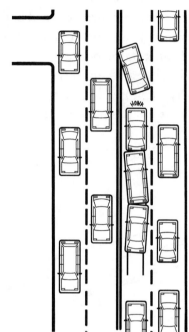

"The Natural Arc Right"

Sometimes called the "Wide Right," this is popular with vegetarians and bongo players. The idea is to listen to your car's natural rhythms, flowing with the curvature of the earth

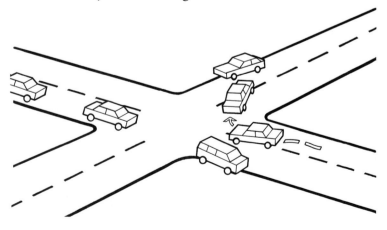

and the road. You allow your car to speak through you. This inevitably leads to a wider arc for the right turn. This turn is not popular with control freaks or drivers in adjacent lanes, especially if these lanes are oncoming traffic lanes.

"The Fake Right, Merge Left Non-Turn"

Another turn which allows you to travel at a reasonable speed even when traffic is moving unreasonably slowly. The "Right Turn Only" Lane opens up, creating a hole in the defensive line. You plunge through the gap, gain impressive yardage as you move down field, then at the last moment you lateral back into the through lanes.

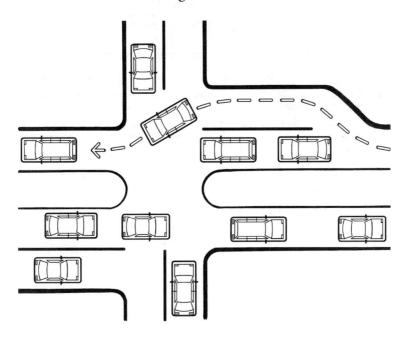

"The Suicide Forced Yield Left"

You're waiting for that magic moment when there's a break in traffic in both directions big enough for you to make that left turn, but it's not happening. So using your own car and body as a STOP sign, you enter the road boldly. Be sure to wave "thank you" as you force the other drivers to let you in by throwing yourself in front of them, counting on their good will not to run into you. Ignore angry honking.

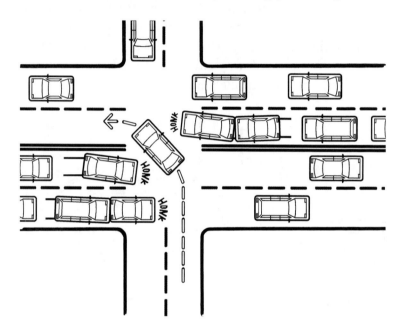

"The Instant Gridlock Intersection Paralyzer"

In this maneuver you weigh the importance of making your left turn (even though there's no space for your car) against the estimated importance of oncoming cross traffic getting through the intersection and conclude that their time is a sacrifice you will have to make.

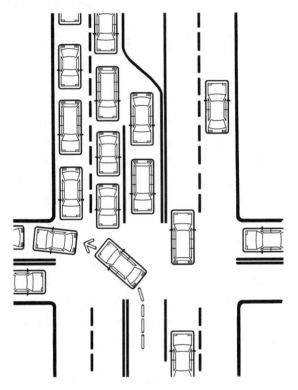

Summary

You may have noticed that the subject of turn signals was not discussed as thoroughly as you might have expected in a chapter titled, "Turn Signals." This is our way of emphasizing how important it is *not* to reveal what you're going to do before you do it. This handbook teaches by example, not by lecturing.

CHAPTER 2

Speed Limits, Einstein's Theory of Relativity, and You

The laws of the road have not yet caught up with our understanding of science. Decades of breathtaking advances in scientific theory have come simultaneously with decades of discouraging stagnation in our development of traffic codes. Nowhere is this disconnect more apparent than in the area of speed limits.

As long ago as 1905, Albert Einstein first introduced his famous Special Theory of Relativity, and in 1915 the General Theory of Relativity, which led to the very useful atomic bomb, among other things. He not only found the equivalent relationship between matter and energy, he proved that distance, time and more importantly speed are ambiguous measurements *relative* to the observer.

Basically, what he was trying to say, in his own, roundabout way, is that speed limits are a crock of sh*t. A traffic cop stopped at the side of the road using antiquated measuring equipment may perceive your speed to be one thing, where the observer in the back seat of your car perceives it to be another.

In the event you are stopped by a traffic officer unaware of these scientific advancements, here are some things you can say in your own defense:

YOU
I was going 85 compared to what? That's *your* perspective. If you consider me to be the reference point, then it was *you* who was going 85. And *you're* supposed to be enforcing the law.

OFFICER
Good point! I never thought of that before. Sorry for the inconvenience. You can go now.

YOU
Just don't let it happen again.

or more specifically:

YOU
Surely you're aware that the earth's surface is rotating at a speed of 25,000 miles per 24 hours, a little more than 1,000 miles per hour. So I was actually traveling at either 1,085 miles an hour or 915 miles an hour, depending on the earth's rotational direction relative to mine. Is that really such a big deal in the cosmic sense of things? Not to mention the earth itself is moving around the sun at a speed of 67,000 miles per hour. So you were going pretty fast yourself, Officer.

OFFICER
Looking at things from that perspective, I *was* going pretty fast. I guess I owe you an apology.

YOU
Don't apologize to me. Apologize to Albert Einstein.

(Note: in order not to overtax the mental capacity of the traffic officer, you may want to skip the speed of our galaxy which moves at 600 kilometers a second, or 1.34 million miles per hour in the direction of the constellation Hydra, and the rate of expansion of the universe itself.)

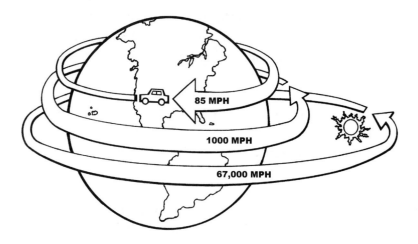

Summary

Studies have shown that the more time you spend on the road, the more likely you are to get into an accident. Common sense tells you that the faster you drive, the less time you spend on the road. It doesn't take a nuclear physicist to deduce that the faster you drive, the fewer accidents you will have.

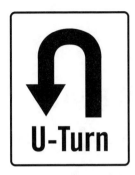

U-Turn

Did You Know?

→ People who are frequently cited for speeding violations are more likely to be involved in accidents, so a good way to avoid accidents is to cut down on speeding tickets by buying a radar detector.

→ Driving 10 m.p.h. over the speed limit will save you only about three minutes on a 30-mile trip. Clearly, if you want to save any reasonable amount of time, you'll have to drive *a lot* faster than that.

→ The truth about speed bumps, usually found in quiet residential areas, is that if you take them fast enough, you don't feel anything at all.

CHAPTER 3

Communicating with Other Drivers: So Much Hostility, So Little Time

The most basic way of communicating with other drivers is with hand signals. Due to advances in technology, we now also have various electronic signals, but hand signals are still the most reliable method. Here are a few of the most commonly used signals that everyone should know:

Left Turn

Right Turn

Stop

Haven't Quite Decided Yet

Is It Raining?

I'm Just Sort of Hanging My Arm Out the Window for No Apparent Reason

Westside

I'm Very Unsatisfied with Your Driving

Establishing a line of communication with other drivers is also important in other situations, like determining the right-of-way at a 4-Way STOP sign. In theory, one driver makes eye contact with another, then waves the other driver through the intersection. In practice, you will *never* use this gesture, since yielding the right-of-way is a sign of weakness, but you should be able to recognize it when another driver uses it.

We communicate to help each other become better drivers. However, moving at the speeds we do while driving, there often isn't time for lengthy discussion. This is why drivers can come across as lacking in social graces. It's not so much that they are insensitive, it's just that they are concise. To be effective, you must compress your critique to the most essential points, a general summation of your key concerns:

What You Want to Say	**What You Do Say**
In my judgment, your last lane change left much to be desired. I feel that your erratic behavior is compromising my safety and the safety of all other drivers so that you may or may not shave three seconds off your commute time.	A**hole!
Hey, buddy, just want to throw you a heads-up: you know that clicking noise you've been hearing for the past eight blocks? That's your turn signal. Many of us use the turn signal to indicate we're about to make a turn, but I've lost confidence that you intend to carry out such a maneuver.	A**hole!
While I recognize that you appear to be lost and as a result are slowing down to try to read street signs and difficult-to-see address numbers, I feel that a better solution for the rest of the drivers on the road would be for you to pull over, stop your car, consult a map, or perhaps call whichever other intellectual giant it is you are trying to visit.	Stupid f**king moron a**hole!

Bumper Stickers: Religion and Politics Are Just the Beginning—You Can Start a Conflict with Another Driver Over Almost Anything

If you feel strongly about something, like politics, an excellent way to persuade others to join you is with a bumper sticker affixed to the rear of your car. A driver in the car behind you sees the name of your candidate and is suddenly moved to vote for that person, especially if the person's name is surrounded with an attractive and patriotic color scheme. You can be an active member of your political party without having to get into all the boring stuff like attending meetings, organizing fund-raisers, and voting.

Similarly, by affixing a religious message to your car, you can easily save the souls of heathens while you get your groceries, or pick up the kids from school, or sneak away from home for an extramarital affair. While you're upstairs in the motel room, your message is working for you in the parking lot below.

You can help tip the balance of a tight playoff series in favor of your team, enhance the reputation of your alma mater, make new friends for your elementary school honor student, and help save the natural resources of our planet, all by simply adding a bumper sticker to your car. This socially conscious driver, for example, is doing his part to clean up the environment:

In addition to the obvious persuasive power of your bumper sticker, it enables you to reach out to other drivers with opposing opinions and/or bumper stickers and initiate the kind of dialog which makes our democracy strong, and our sports rivalries spirited. By exchanging verbal or even physical retorts, you can transform a dreary driving errand into an exciting debate, while meeting other drivers you'd normally never encounter.

Caution: As soon as you put a bumper sticker on your car, you become a representative of the politician or deity you invoke. In a tight election you never know when the driver in the car next to yours is an undecided voter.

Alert: The highly sought-after "undecided" voter is very impressionable, a person whose opinions are subject to sudden change by political advertisements, shiny colors, Fox News, or your driving behavior. If you're unable to resist the temptation to cut off other drivers, zip around them with illegal turns, engage in tailgating and other standard techniques described in this book, you may want to put the bumper sticker of your candidate's opponent on your car. Or you may want to advertise a different religion from your own.

Summary

Just because someone doesn't have a bumper sticker that says, "How am I driving?" with an 800 number to call, doesn't mean that person doesn't want to know. Assume that all drivers really want to know, and the ones without a phone number want to know right away.

CHAPTER 4

Intimidating Pedestrians

There are so many annoying things about pedestrians. They infringe upon your right to drive at the speed you feel most comfortable. Their actions are sudden and unpredictable, bringing chaos into an otherwise orderly ecosystem of automobiles and traffic arteries. Even the *word* "pedestrian" is annoying. Walking is not complicated enough to require so many syllables. Plus, it sounds like "equestrian," which is also an extremely annoying word.

When considering the so-called rights of pedestrians, a good question to ask is: Who pays for the roads you travel on? Who pays to construct them? Who pays to maintain them? The answer, which should be painfully obvious whenever you fill up your tank with gas at a price unreasonably inflated by taxes is: You do! And yet you are forced to share your roads with pedestrians. And *they* always get the right of way! Why is that? You're bigger, you're stronger, you're faster. It is, not surprisingly, because of the espresso-drinking fascists at the DMV.

So you have to share. But who are these "pedestrians"? They may look ordinary, but a brooding, violent anger inside them is just waiting for an excuse to erupt. They already hate you. Because you're different. Because you're driving a car, and they're not. So when you've been waiting patiently for what seems like hours to make that left turn, and finally there's a tiny break in traffic and you're about to pull out, you look ahead and there they are: walking slowly, slowly across in front of you, staring cruelly into your eyes, flaunting their right of way.

Don't they realize how unhealthy all that walking is? How much unnecessary strain they put on their tendons and ligaments? It's an insult to the progress of the industrial revolution. Our great-great-grandfathers weren't crushed by large pieces of machinery at unregulated assembly lines at the Ford motor company so that you could walk around everywhere. *They died so you don't have to walk.*

How to Deal with Pedestrians

1. Don't make eye contact. It only encourages them.

2. Don't take it personally, it's not you they hate, they were miserable failures, seething with undifferentiated rage long before you ever appeared, speeding towards their crosswalk.

3. Whatever you do, don't slow down. They will take it as a sign of weakness, and walk all over you, so to speak.

At one time, it was thought that pedestrians were smart enough to figure out when to walk and when not to walk simply by looking at the traffic lights, but after a while it became clear that this was too complicated, so "Walk" and "Don't Walk" signs were introduced. Unfortunately, interpreting these signs was still too difficult for most pedestrians, so they were replaced by simple pictures which show a stick figure walking to encourage the pedestrian to walk, and a hand upraised in the traditional "stop" position to discourage walking. Sadly, many pedestrians are still confused.

Alert: Common sense tells you that if pedestrians cross the street against the light, you can run them over. However, the sad truth is if you do, you can still get in trouble, even though you have the right of way! This is because pedestrians are above the law. They can walk under the influence, they can walk without a license, they can walk as fast or as slow as they want, the only thing they can get in trouble for is jaywalking, and they never do.

Another example of these discriminatory policies is that while pedestrians are given preferential access to automobile roads (i.e. "crosswalks"), drivers are prohibited from driving on sidewalks, as we are reminded by the rigid disciplinarians at the *DMV* who write, "Do not drive on a sidewalk." (*California DMV Driver's Handbook,* p. 20)

Because life is so full of irony it's important to remember that at any moment you yourself can become a pedestrian by getting out of your car, at which point all your hostility towards pedestrians should immediately be transformed into hostility towards cars and drivers. As a pedestrian you'll need to know how to deal with those scumbag drivers who think they own the road.

How to Get Across a Crosswalk

1. Show no fear. If you show any hesitation, a good driver will pick up on this, and you're not going anywhere.

2. Travel in herds. There is safety in numbers. A group or crowd can easily become a mob. Drivers know this.

3. Look the other way so the driver thinks you don't see him. (Only works under the bold assumption the driver cares whether you see him or not.)

4. If you do establish eye contact with a driver, he will sometimes wave you across the intersection. This means you can walk across with confidence. *Alert:* Make sure you understand the exact meaning of that wave. There

are several gestures that drivers make which appear similar, but have different meanings:

"I see you, and will slow down until you have safely crossed the intersection."

"I'm using expressive hand gestures to help communicate an idea to the person on the other end of this cell phone."

"There's an annoying insect in my car which I'm trying to crush against my windshield, and I'm not paying any attention to the road."

"I've got this uncontrollable twitch in my arm, which causes my hand to wave back and forth in a manner which in most circumstances would, but in this circumstance definitely does not, *indicate I intend to let you cross the road."*

Terrorism, Crimes Against Humanity and Bike Lanes

What a pleasure it is to share the road with bikers! They serve as a constant reminder to drivers of how healthy and fit we could all be. How pure and wholesome, how ecofriendly. By following their example, we could diminish our dependence on foreign oil and become more responsible guardians of the limited resources of our planet. They are a virtual model of the people we could, but never will become. Yes, it's a pleasure and an honor to merely be in their presence, which we are a lot of the time because they're constantly blocking the goddamn road. A**holes!

Seriously, what are these people thinking? Invading the limited space of our streets and highways, making left turns in the middle of busy intersections. Wouldn't they be happier in a park or nature preserve, eating tofu and riding around in circles amidst the poppies and the trees? Wouldn't they rather take their holistic bikes made entirely of recycled soda cans (not that they'd ever drink soda or anything else packaged in aluminum) into the mountains to frolic amongst the deer and the antelope?

The truth is bicyclists miss the whole point of the invention of the wheel, which is to free us of the burden of using our own muscles to get places. The wheel was invented to be placed on cars, which had previously been something of a disappointment. Putting wheels on bicycles is a giant step backwards in the march of technology. But it happened, and now we have bike lanes.

Vocabulary Alert

Bike lane: 1. A lane which need not be marked, basically anywhere the biker feels comfortable riding, which inevitably takes up half of the actual driving lane, so it's impossible for the biker and the driver to coexist peacefully. 2. A naked land grab engineered by the Bicycle Manufacturing Industry to deprive drivers of their ancestral heritage.

Oh, and One More Thing

All those special bright clothes and reflective patches they wear so we can see them. If they really want us to see them, they should put their bikes in an SUV and climb behind the wheel. *Then* we'd see them.

Summary for Pedestrians and Cyclists

There is currently an acute shortage of pedestrians and cyclists in Germany, France, Australia, and several other Communist nations where you'd be greatly appreciated. No, seriously: please leave our country.

Summary for Drivers

Most cyclists can be coaxed off the road by skillfully tossing healthy foods like wheat grass and tofu in front of them.

CHAPTER 5

The Good Driver Management Guide

As we have mentioned, one of the most dangerous hazards you will find on the road is the legendary "good driver." This egregiously mislabeled phenomenon obeys no laws of intuition, common sense or efficiency. From the perspective of reason, his behavior may appear erratic or absurd.

If you are ever in a situation when a good driver is present on the road, you must be vigilant. On the other hand, many of his actions can be predicted if you know what to look for. The simple mind of the good driver will cling to any bit of instruction he can find, like a lost child, an aimless, wandering spirit. These good drivers are compliant, like trained circus animals who have no ability to reason or think on their own.

Note Similarities

Good Driver   *Trained Circus Animals*

The Pathology of the Good Driver

If you want to know how fast they will be traveling at a given time, look around and see if there are any signs with numbers on them. If you see a sign with a number on it, it is quite likely that the problematic good driver will be traveling at a speed exactly equal to that number. If there are any words posted on nearby signs, pay particular attention to what they say, as the good drivers on the road are very likely to react reflexively to any one of these instructions, be it "YIELD", "SLOW," "Shop at K-mart," "Check out the new *Friends* spin-off, *Joey*," "Vote Larouche," or even "STOP."

More Things to Look Out for

When a traffic light turns Yellow:	Be prepared to *swerve* around them as they are likely to stop instead of accelerate reasonably through the intersection.
At a crosswalk:	Here they are also likely to stop suddenly, just for pedestrians. Use extreme caution.
In certain weather conditions:	In the mind of the good driver there seems to be some sort of relationship between rain, ice, snow and fog, and an uncontrollable urge to drive slowly.
In school zones:	Likely to decelerate dramatically for no reason, possibly because they're still afraid of the teachers who broke their spirit in the first place. Anyway it's not up to us to try to figure out why they do these things, but rather to be informed and aware.

Summary for Good Drivers

We're sorry we've been making fun of you. We're just jealous because you're so goddamn perfect.

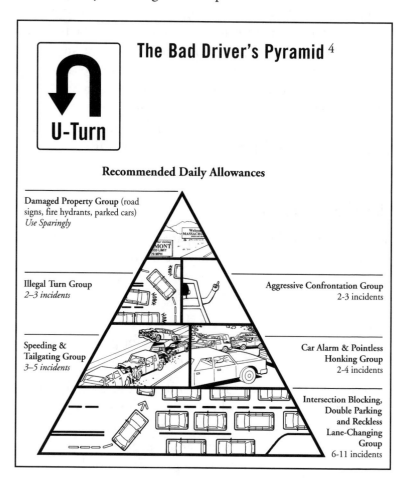

The Bad Driver's Pyramid [4]

Recommended Daily Allowances

Damaged Property Group (road signs, fire hydrants, parked cars) *Use Sparingly*

Illegal Turn Group *2–3 incidents*

Aggressive Confrontation Group 2-3 incidents

Speeding & Tailgating Group *3–5 incidents*

Car Alarm & Pointless Honking Group 2-4 incidents

Intersection Blocking, Double Parking and Reckless Lane-Changing Group 6-11 incidents

[4] We recognize The Bad Driver's Pyramid has not been updated to coincide with the new Food Pyramid issued by the FDA. We also recognize that they spent a lot of time at the FDA redesigning the Pyramid instead of determining if new drugs they're approving have uncomfortable side effects like organ failure and sudden death. We further recognize that the new design totally sucks, and the chances that anyone will pay attention to it are even less than they were before. So we'll use the old design, and see you at Carl's Jr.

Bluffing Your Way to a License

The Written Test: Good News—You Can Get Six Questions Wrong! Bad News: There Are More Than Six Questions

Now that you've been driving for a while, you may want to have your abilities recognized by getting a fancy degree known as a "driver's license." You may also have to submit to this invasion of your privacy when you renew your license, or when it has been unjustly stripped away by police officers who took the *DMV Driver's Handbook* way too literally. This dehumanizing process typically starts with the written test. If you already have a license, you should still read this chapter because *(note to publisher: before publication remind authors to make up some bullsh*t about why everyone should read this chapter to be inserted here).*

Until *The Bad Driver's Handbook* replaces the *DMV Driver's Handbook* as the nationally recognized standard, taking the *DMV Written Test* should be considered by all drivers. However, memorizing the misinformation in their handbook does nothing to prepare you for the situations you will face in the real world.

Therefore, we suggest you study for and pass the *Bad Driver's Written Test* as well, to insure you will be a safe and predictable citizen of the road.

In addition to being a more accurate evaluation of driving knowledge, our written test has several other advantages. While it is the same in that you can get six questions wrong and still pass, our test has fewer questions, to be specific, six questions. It also comes with a more positive, feel-good, confidence-building attitude that is notably lacking in the other test. But first, let's see if we can't unlearn a little of the propaganda we've been force-fed by the freedom-hating fanatics at the DMV with a brief study guide:

Road Signs—The Hidden Truth

The often-misunderstood "YIELD" sign, which has some other meaning you might want to know solely to pass *their* written test, in any real world situation actually means:

> → "Under no circumstances should you ever YIELD to anyone."

Similarly, the oddly-worded "NO U-TURN" sign in practical application means:

> → "Look both ways for police officers, if you don't see any, go ahead and make the U-turn."

Then there is the always confusing 4-WAY STOP sign. The rule in the Communist-inspired *DMV Driver's Handbook* states, "When two cars approach, the second car to come to a complete stop yields to the first car to come to a complete stop." This confusing and long-winded rule is more clearly understood when stated more simply:

→ At a 4-WAY STOP SIGN the right-of-way *always* goes to the car which doesn't stop at all.

In the more complex situation when three or four cars stop at the same time,

→ The biggest, most intimidating vehicle is granted the right-of-way. If all cars are similarly large and intimidating, the right-of-way is granted to the vehicle playing the *loudest music.*

Now that you've been rescued from the fantasy world of the fascist *DMV Driver's Handbook*, it's time to take the *Bad Driver's Written Test*. If you're not sure you're ready, remember you can get up to six questions wrong.

The Bad Driver's Written Test

1. A double yellow line, which splits off to become two double yellow lines, with a broken yellow line alternating inside-outside with the solid line every two hundred yards on each of the yellow line pairs on either side of a broken red line in the center, beneath a flashing yellow light means:
A) Weave cautiously back and forth from lane to lane.
B) Get off the road and find another one with less complicated markings.
C) Wing it.

☺ *Good job for trying! We can't get them all right.*

2. If a traffic signal light is not working because of an electrical power failure, you should:

A) Proceed through the intersection as though the light were green.

B) Get out of your vehicle and direct traffic until a real traffic officer arrives to take over.

C) Do anything you damn well please, since law and order no longer exists.

☺ *Hey, it's all right, lots of people get confused by multiple choice questions.*

3. You may legally use your horn to

A) Alert another driver of your presence to avoid an accident.

B) Inform another driver that he's an a**hole.

C) Inform the residents of your friend's neighborhood that you are here to pick her up and that you are pissed off that she isn't ready.

D) Punctuate an especially important moment in a song you're listening to.

☺ *So you're not so good at this test. Maybe you're a lot better at something else, like balloon animals.*

4. The "Exit Only" lane on a freeway may also be used as a passing lane when

A) you are in a big hurry

B) you feel like being a big jerk

C) it's rush hour

D) you're having a bad day

☺ *If everyone were smart, there would be no context for appreciating how smart other people are.*

5. This question is a freebie for trying so hard to answer the previous four questions. All you have to do is circle A) or B). *[Not C)]*

A) Swerve into another lane.

B) Play it by ear.

C) Remember, don't pick this one. The correct answer is A) or B)

☺ *Actually, the answer was A) or B), but it was kind of a confusing question, so it's OK that you missed it.*

6. Essay Question for Teenage Drivers: Answer *one* of the following *two* questions:

Getting your license can be a great opportunity to assist in the daily chores and activities of your family.

1) List five things you could do once you get your license to help your family with its multiple burdens and responsibilities.

2) List five things you will *actually* do once you get your license, which will in no way ease your family's burdens and responsibilities, but will in fact increase the number and severity of the ones they already have.

☺ *Congratulations! You passed!*

CHAPTER 7

Driving Instructors: Did You Know Most Driving Instructors Are From Countries Where the Right-of-Way Is Determined by Armed Conflict?

Do you ever read the newspapers and wonder why we're bombing the hell out of this or that weaker nation? Self defense, of course: if we didn't bomb their country, immigrants would have no reason to come here and become driving instructors, and our roads would become very dangerous.

But we are a welcoming society. We encourage people of all origins and ethnicities to come to our country, especially if they're willing to teach our psychotic teenagers to drive.

However, not all driving instructors are called to the profession in this way.

Reasons Someone Might Become a Driving Instructor Other Than to Avoid Being Carpet-Bombed by the U.S. Military

1. We've destroyed their country's economy in some other way.
2. Can't afford overdose of sleeping pills.
3. Unique combination of altruism and self-loathing.

There are good reasons why a driving instructor is a calmer and more confident teacher than a family member.

1. It's not his car.
2. He doesn't know you.
3. He's heavily medicated.
4. He's driven the Kabul-Peshawar Highway and lived to tell about it.
5. He knows other drivers will clear a path for you because of the huge neon sign that says, "Student Driver."
6. It's not his car.

So you should definitely take advantage of this experienced professional. But perhaps you are reading this chapter not because you are a student, but because you are a driving instructor seeking advice on how to communicate with Americans, especially teenage Americans. Here are a few translations:

Key Phrases	**Translation**
Slow down.	Hey Dude, chill out on the gizass pedal, yo.
Stop knocking over bikers.	Hey, stizop hittin' the cycles, yo.
Watch out!	Hey, yo, watch out, yo!

Now that you're comfortable communicating with students, you want to strike a balance between what can be taught and what a driver has to learn on her own, without limiting her unique driving personality. We don't want to create a whole nation of people who all drive the same way. How boring would that be? What a road sign means to one person may be completely different from what it means to another. A good road sign is like a good poem—direct, concise, but subject to multiple interpretations. You wouldn't tell someone exactly how to interpret Shakespeare, so don't tell them exactly how to interpret a "DO NOT ENTER" sign. Have faith that your student will interpret the sign in a way that is correct for her, and support her in that decision.

Chapter Summary for Driving Instructors

Ever since *Time Magazine* ran its featured cover story, "America's 100 Sexiest Driving Instructors," many people have gotten the wrong idea about what it's really like to live this kind of lifestyle. Sure, there's the parties, drugs, and unrestrained sexual overindulgence side of it, but it's also a lot of hard work. It's a glamorous job, but it's still a job.

Chapter Summary for Immigration Policy Makers

Immigration is such a tough, profound moral dilemma. Clearly we don't want a bunch of people who look different from us running wild in our country, which we rightfully stole from people who look different from us by killing most of them, but damned if they don't come in handy sometimes.

Chapter Summary for Driving Students

Driving instructors have so much to teach you besides just driving. They have a unique perspective on life that many Westerners don't have. It's that "live every day to the fullest, because it might be your last" kind of existential liberation that can only be achieved by becoming a driving instructor, or eating every wild berry or mushroom you see growing anywhere.

CHAPTER 8

Making Your Visit to the DMV Successful

It's not that hard to have a successful visit to the DMV if you are prepared, patient and determined. First make sure you have all the documentation you need, including every driver's license and car registration you've ever had, proof of insurance and transfers of ownership.

OK. Got it all? Now drive to the DMV, get out of your car, enter the building. You will note that the DMV is highly organized, and broken down into the various areas associated with the different tasks you might be coming to address. For example, say you want to sell your car. You must go to Window 18, "Transfer of Ownership" which is found on page 149.

Please go now to page 149. Thank you.

CHAPTER 9

Driving with Your Parents: Nothing That 10 Years of Intensive Psychotherapy Can't Partially Mend

Drivers who already have a license: DO NOT ENTER this chapter.

WRONG WAY, GO BACK
SEVERE TIRE DAMAGE

You don't want to know what's going on in that car in the lane next to yours with the teenage driver and her parent.

Instead, follow our DETOUR signs at the bottom of the page, which like any real world DETOUR has multiple signs at first which will do an excellent job of leading you away from the path you were following, but slowly decrease in frequency and then abandon you in the middle of nowhere, because the people who put up the DETOUR signs are really only paid to keep you from going where you want to go, and don't actually give a damn where you end up, as long as it's not the place you were going.

DETOUR → DETOUR → DETOUR →

OK. Now that all the older drivers have gone off to follow the DETOUR and are in the process of getting lost, it's just you teenagers who are reading this.

First, let's start with a little *bad news.* Driving with your parents is not always as fun as it sounds. As eager as you may be to spend 20 to 50 hours bonding with your parents (depending on the specific level of sadism practiced by your state's DMV), these special times can be tense.

Your parents do not see you as the competent, responsible citizen of the road that you are. In fact *this* is how they see you:

Your parents don't remember that they too were once teenagers learning to drive. Or even worse, maybe they *do* remember. In any case, it can be dangerous to have a nervous parent sitting next to you. They could grab the wheel, they could scream, or just be so annoying you lose control of the delicately small part of your attention span you're able to allocate to the task of driving. So you need to gently reassure them that everything is going to be all right.

DETOUR →   DETOUR →   DETOUR ↓

Things to Say to Make Your Parents More Comfortable

"Don't worry, Mom, this isn't my first time behind the wheel—I've been taking your car out late at night for some time now. My friends have been driving your car, too. We've been learning together. This little minivan can really fly!"

"Dad, I've been doing much more dangerous things than driving. For years."

"I've been carefully studying how you drive for a very long time, Dad, and I promise I'll do exactly as you do."

"This car has air bags, right?"

Now that your parents are relaxed and confident of your abilities, you can begin the magical process of family bonding that results from having a parent screaming into your ear every two seconds for an hour and a half.

At first your mother may not fully believe you see the car directly in front of you, especially if it's slowing down. She's trying to be supportive, but in the haste of the moment it sometimes comes out a little curt. So try not to be offended. Here are a few examples of how to interpret parental instructions:

What Your Parents Say in Haste	**What They Really Mean**
STOP!!	Not too fast, dear. There's a tricky intersection up ahead, and it's best not to cross it when the light is red.

↙ DETOUR ↖   ↗ DETOUR →   → DETOUR ←

What Your Parents Say in Haste	What They Really Mean
WATCH OUT!!	I know you're going to stop for that truck, because I trust you.
AIEEEEEEE!!	That's OK, even the best drivers have trouble seeing pedestrians.
ARRRGGGHHHH!!	You're doing great! I never really liked this car. It's time to get a new one, anyway.

Teaching Your Parents How to Be Good Driving Instructors

Although this is not well known, a high percentage of accidents involving teenagers are due to embarrassment caused by parents. For safety reasons, you will want to try and help reduce your parents' tendency to embarrass you, as much as possible, with some instructional guidelines. The *good news* is that even if you only have a permit, basically, you have a license. Congratulations! But if your parents are going to be hanging around while you drive, you might want to teach them a little about not being total dorks around your friends.

On the other hand, if you manage to convince your parents to ride in the trunk of your car, and wait there while you go to parties, the whole problem can be avoided. If your parents don't want to ride in the trunk, they can ride in the car with you if they wear plain brown bags over their heads. If they insist, you can even cut eye holes in the bags.

↗ DETOUR ←   DETOUR →   → DETOUR ↑

Listening to Your Parents' Safety Lectures—Try to Stay Awake, Look Alert

You may notice a distinct disconnect between how your parents are teaching you to drive and how they actually drive themselves. This is because they're hypocrites. It's no reason to hate them, you will be a hypocrite one day, too. It's part of growing up. So you're being trained to drive by vicious hypocrites. Just nod and try to look serious. Remember, they won't be driving with you forever.

Safety Tip

Entering the freeway for the first time is a very important moment in a driver's training process. As you merge onto this dangerous road, turn to your parent driving trainer, stare maniacally deep into their eyes, and ask, "What kind of car am I going to be getting?" Do not break the stare to look back at the freeway until you get the correct answer.

Did You Know?

In some states the law says that a teenager cannot take the road test without first logging 50 hours driving with her parents. There is also an amendment to the Constitution of the United States banning cruel and unusual punishment. Clearly, one of these laws must be changed. (Considering your luck, it will be the latter.)

↖ DETOUR ↗   ↗ DETOUR ↘   → DETOUR ↗

Chapter Summary

If your parents are still giving you a hard time about your driving, still screaming and grabbing at the wheel every little time you brush up against another car or a tree, you can try some of the lines you've learned from them, like, "You know, I can turn this car around *right now* and we can go home. Is that what you want?"

DETOUR ↖   ↗DETOUR →   NOT A THRU STREET

Teaching Your Teen to Drive—Nothing That 10 Years of Reconstructive Surgery Can't Minimally Improve

What a proud moment for Mom and Dad, when your teenager comes bounding in the front door, waving her newly won Learner's Permit! And you, being a good parent, are equally excited by the prospect of driving in endless circles around the neighborhood with an inexperienced, dangerous novice at the wheel for 20 to 50 hours.

It seems like only yesterday she was a carefree youngster, totally lacking in purpose and maturity, unable to focus on one thing for more 20 seconds at a time, incapable of performing the simplest acts of responsibility.

Wait a minute, that *was* yesterday.

But never mind. The same authorities who have driven your state to the brink of bankruptcy have determined that your child is ready to drive.

The best way to teach your teen to drive is to lead by example. Even the DMV acknowledges this. According to them,

"Children of every age often imitate their parents' behavior." [5] You may notice this in the way they dress, the music they listen to, and the things they do for fun. This means for the immediate period before, during and after your child gets her license, you will have to significantly *modify* your driving.

To be an effective driving instructor you must earn the respect of your trainee. So you'll have to appear (and this is a word you should use as frequently as possible) "cool." It's not so hard. When your young driver makes a good turn, give him a "high five." Bust out the old bell bottoms and put on some hip "shades." Bring some of your favorite rock 'n roll to play while teaching: anything by The Captain and Tennile or Sonny and Cher.

Cool Parent Instructor

To further cement your relationship, you can tell him about the time you were almost "nailed" by "the fuzz." Now your young driver is no longer embarrassed to be in the car with you. He might even want to drive around to his school and show you off!

---

[5] State of California DMV Parent-Teen Training Guide, page 4.

How to Give Instructions

Keep your voice CALM!!

Tell her where you want something done *before* telling her what you want her to do: Instead of, "Turn right at the next corner," say: "At the next corner, turn right." If you say "turn right" first, your teen may react too quickly and turn right into the side of the house she's passing the moment you say "turn right." This would be *your* fault. Similarly, phrase the following instructions exactly as below:

When the light turns green, go.

When there's an opening, change lanes.

At the next STOP sign, stop.

At the next Exit, get off the freeway.

You also have to be careful about how and when you use the word "right." Here is an example of the kind of conversation you *don't* want to have:

YOU
Up at the corner, turn left.

YOUR TEENAGER
So you want me to turn left?

YOU
Right.

YOUR TEENAGER
OK, I'll turn right.

YOU
No! I want you to turn left.

YOUR TEENAGER
But you just *said* "turn right."

YOU
No. Turn *left!*

YOUR TEENAGER
Left?

YOU
Right!

Below are some handy alternatives to use instead of "right":

1. "Bingo!"
2. "Precisely"
3. "Correct"
4. "Correct-o-mundo"
5. "Indubitably"
6. "Oh yeah, baby!"
7. "Fo' shizzle my nizzle."

Good News

Someday you and your teen will look back on this experience with nostalgia and hearty laughter.

Bad News

That day is not today.

Establishing Rules and Boundaries for Your Teenager, and Other Comforting Hallucinations

You want to establish rules and boundaries that are reasonable. This way you're able to maintain the little bit of control you still have over their lives by instituting a set of rules they may actually follow.

Reasonable Rules
1. No doing homework while driving.
2. No driving to the library with friends in the car.
3. No listening to NPR while driving.
4. No sight-seeing expeditions to museums and historical landmarks.

Unreasonable Rules
1. No driving after 2:00 A.M.
2. No using the car to ditch school.
3. No letting unlicensed friends drive the car.
4. No selling the family car for drug money.

We all make occasional mistakes, often when we're young. It's important that your teenager knows that you're on her side, especially when it comes to drugs and alcohol. If you show understanding you can prevent a mistake from becoming a tragedy. Here are a couple of things you can say to your teen to show you're on her side:

"If you're ever drunk at a party and need a ride home, call *any time* and I will pick you up. And you will be grounded for the rest of your life."

"If you're ever at a party and your date is drunk, call any time and we will pick you up, and your father will kill your date. And you will be grounded for the rest of your life."

Now you can be confident that they will turn to you in a moment of crisis.

Did You Know?

It doesn't have to be you who sits with your kid as she learns to drive. Just a licensed driver over the age of 25. Is there a relative who owes you a lot of money? Is there a local homeless person who may be swayed to drive around with her by the persuasive power of a handle of Vodka? Perhaps a sleazy neighbor who might risk his life just to be in her presence?

Summary

If you *are* going to be the one to teach her to drive, it's a good idea to clock in as many instructional hours as possible on family vacations, where you'll be fighting anyway.

CHAPTER 11

Bribes, Threats, and Other Secrets to Passing Your Road Test

There are all sorts of ways to improve your chances of passing your road test other than the overrated strategy of being a good driver. Driving Examiners are not machines, they are just like real people, subject to mood swings, bouts of poor judgment, prejudice, temptation, fear, or the forgiving euphoria which comes from a large dose of Prozac which could potentially find its way into her coffee.

But in case she didn't drink the coffee, here are some other:

Ways to Set Your Driving Examiner at Ease

DO

Break the ice with a joke or two. Remember, your Driving Examiner wants to know who you are as a person, not just as a driver. As you approach your first red light, give a panicked look and say:

"How do you stop this thing?! Ha, ha! Just kidding!"

If your Driving Examiner doesn't laugh, you may have to tell another joke:

"I was so nervous before this test I didn't think I'd make it over here, but six shots of bourbon later, I'm good to go!"

Safety Alert
→ Remember, even though you might joke about it, it's *never* safe to actually drive when you're nervous.

After you've told a few good jokes, your Driving Examiner knows you're not just a good driver, but also full of life, wit and charm, which could be a decisive factor in an otherwise mediocre driving test.

DON'T
Be too self-absorbed. Nobody likes a narcissist. Show that you are *genuinely interested* in your Driving Examiner by asking *probing personal questions.* It's important to keep your Examiner focused on your lively conversation, rather than the details of the actual driving test, especially if you feel you're not doing too well on the driving.

Good Personal Questions to Ask Your Driving Examiner

"How old are you?"

"How much do you weigh?"

"Wow, this must be a lousy job—what do they pay you for this? Not enough, I bet!!"

"Don't you just hate pedestrians? Sometimes I want to— BAM! plow right though 'em, you know?"

DO
Choose the right CD to play during your road test. Driving Examiners love to listen to music while they work, wouldn't

you? But what CD to choose? Of course you'd like to pick one best suited to your particular Examiner, but since you won't know who that is beforehand, it's best to bring standard crowd pleasers generally enjoyed by most people, like Snoop Doggy Dog, Kid Rock, or Insane Clown Posse. If you notice a positive reaction, sing along! And encourage her to sing along also. Now you're having a good time!

Once you've established a personal rapport, it's time to demonstrate your advanced driving skills and the agility of your vehicle.

Ways to Impress Your Driving Examiner

Your Examiner needs to know that if you have to accelerate suddenly to avoid an accident, or stop on a dime, your machine is capable and you are prepared to handle the emergency.

Start by asking, "See any cops? Me neither! Hold on!" Now floor it! If you can go zero to sixty in under five seconds, you'll be sure to gain a few extra points on the test. Once you've hit sixty, slam on those brakes and show off how quickly you can bring the vehicle to a dead stop. Now everyone's in a good mood—adrenaline is pumping and you're giving your Examiner more fun than she's had in a week. (After all, she wouldn't be a Driving Examiner if she didn't enjoy a little excitement.)

If you think you may have lost some points by driving errors, you can offset those losses by demonstrating

Advanced Skills

DO

After you've demonstrated the traditional "10 and 2" steering technique, which any idiot can do, display some creativity with the impressive "3 and 9 crossover" or the "12 o'clock single hand" grip, or the champion of them all . . . the "no-handed 6 o'clock knee" technique.

DO

If you're having trouble keeping up a conversation with your Examiner, *make a phone call.* Show that you can drive safely and manage complex affairs at the same time.

DON'T

Wear a seat belt. Wearing a seat belt suggests you lack confidence. It will make your Driving Examiner nervous.

Leaving On a High Note

First impressions may be important, but last impressions are even more important, especially if your first impression wasn't so great. Here are some parting lines which will help:

"In sum, I'd just like to say that this has been as much of a pleasure for me as it has been for you."

"Good luck! I'm sure you'll find a better job one day."

"You know when I ran that red light, it was only because you were distracting me."

Chapter Summary

Passing your road test on your first try is like having sex on your first date: a much more meaningful experience if you wait until you and the Department of Motor Vehicles have developed a closer relationship.

Where the Hell Did You Learn to Drive?

The question, "Where the Hell did you learn to drive?" is one that a bad driver can expect to hear many times over the course of a lifetime. Since you've been given this question in advance, there's no excuse not to have a clever, well-crafted response ready at hand, like any good politician would.

Try the Dick Cheney: "Go f**k yourself."

Of course if you're not on the floor of the United States Senate, you can be a lot less restrained.

CHAPTER 12

Persuading Your Parents to Buy You a Car, or Trading Up by Totaling the One You're Driving Now

Because your parents don't understand you or care about you as a human being, they are probably not planning to give you the car you deserve. In fact, they're probably not planning to give you any kind of a car. If they can be persuaded to give you one, it's unlikely to be the one you deserve, but instead, in an act of cruelty and selfishness, that old clunker that they've been driving when they get a newer model for themselves. But this *great country* was not made by people who accepted defeat easily. It is your duty to yourself, your family, your community, and yes, your country to do everything in your power to make your parents buy you a great car.

Your Main Talking Points

Civic Duty

Remind your parents of their obligations as citizens. They may not realize it, but this is not only an issue of compassion and basic decency, but a legal issue as well. Pick up any DMV handbook and you're likely to see something like:

→ Driving is a right, not a privilege.

(We're paraphrasing here, but the language is very similar. Anyway, that's the general idea.)

Furthermore, this right is established firmly in the Constitution of the United States, a document you should have on hand during all family discussions on this subject. When you first make the Constitutional argument, your parents will most likely demand to know where in the Constitution it says they have to buy you a car. Fortunately, the relevant language is in the most well-known section, the Preamble, which states,

"We the people of the United States, in order to form a more perfect union, establish justice, insure domestic tranquility, provide for the common defense, promote the general welfare, and secure the blessings of liberty to ourselves and our posterity, do ordain and establish this Constitution for the United States of America."

Obviously, the key phrase here is "secure the blessings of liberty to ourselves and our posterity." Having a great car is one of the basic blessings of liberty, or as stated in the Declaration of Independence, an "inalienable right." These documents were clearly written by people who were not only political visionaries, but also good parents who knew the value of providing their children with great automobiles. All this, in combination with judicial rulings in Anderson v. State of Wisconsin, Douglas v. Board of Transportation, and Tyson v. Hollyfield, is certainly overwhelming legal precedent for your claim.

Now we can move on to what *kind* of a car you should have.

The answer is: an expensive new car. This may not be what your parents have in mind. So, once again, you will have to explain why. There are several good reasons. Like:

You Care Deeply About the Environment. The newer a car is, the more likely it is to have advanced technology to reduce toxic emissions which could damage our fragile ecosystem. (You don't have to disclose your secret desire for a Chevy Suburban until it's already been agreed upon that a new car is in order. Right now we're establishing that the car must be new and expensive. We'll get into specifics about which make and model later. It's essential to take this debate one step at a time.)

You're Concerned About Safety. It's amazing how much the American automobile industry has improved the safety of its products in the last five years. There are airbags, passenger compartment reinforcement, anti-lock brakes, not to mention that the faster your car is, the better you can maneuver out of potentially dangerous situations. A safe car like a brand new Pontiac Firebird or Mustang GT convertible is essential to protect you and your passengers. You can point out statistics about how many teenage drivers are involved in accidents, so no matter how careful you are, you'll probably have one too. Do they want you to be in an unsafe car when you have yours?

Your Growth as a Human Being. This would be a good time to bring up Ivan Pavlov's Theories of Conditioned Reflex. Like Pavlov's dog, you can be positively or negatively conditioned by rewards or punishment. "I've worked so hard to get my license, if you don't buy me a Corvette, I'll have it ingrained in my subconscious psyche that hard work leads to nothing, I'll salivate at completely unrelated stimuli, and I'll be inclined not to work hard ever again. Doesn't anybody here give a damn about science?!"

Teaching Responsibility. There's nothing like owning an expensive new car to teach the important life lessons of responsibility to a young person like yourself. Remind them of how irresponsible you currently are, citing specific examples if necessary (it probably won't be), and how essential a new car would be to your developing maturity.

While the compelling logic of these arguments should be obvious to any impartial observer, your parents may need more convincing. That's why it's a good idea to have some *personal stories* in reserve:

> YOU
> Did you hear about Jennifer? She totaled the ugly car her parents made her drive because she was too embarrassed to drive it on the main road and drove it on dangerous side streets instead.

> PARENT
> (HORRIFIED) Is she all right?

> YOU
> Well, I wouldn't want to be her.

Or you could try this:

> YOU
> Patrick almost got this great summer job!
> But he didn't have a car, and somebody else who did have a car got there first.

Or possibly:

> YOU
> Roger didn't get to go to the coolest party in town last weekend because he didn't have a car, and had to stay home and study all night instead!

Now your parents are really convinced. However, they still may not be able to afford the car you deserve, even though they realize how necessary it is. It's up to you to go the extra mile, to be flexible, to compromise. Here's a list of things you can offer to do without as your contribution to the family effort to buy you a car:

Things You're Willing to Sacrifice

Textbooks
Furniture
Tutor
Piano lessons
Green vegetables
Trips to visit relatives in other states

Now that they're impressed by how much you're willing to contribute, it's time to remind them of all the things they've done wrong as parents. You should have been keeping track of these things, but if you haven't, take some time to go back over your whole life, especially every moment of unhappiness which could be directly or indirectly blamed on your parents. This may take a while, but it's worth the effort. When they're feeling sufficiently guilty, hold up a picture of the car you want and say, "You know, we can forget about all this, if you like..." (Be sure and reserve a couple of instances of your parents' bad behavior for future negotiations.)

Chapter Summary

If after all this, your parents still won't buy you a car, you might consider the possibility that they *truly* cannot afford it. This doesn't mean they hate you. They probably just don't like you all that much.

Intermediate Skills Development

CHAPTER 13

Hitting a Parked Car, the Overcrowded Lifeboat, and Other Moral Dilemmas

It's an all-too familiar story, and if it hasn't already happened to you, one day it will. You're driving along, or maneuvering into a tight parking spot, and CRUNCH, another car seemingly leaps into your path from out of nowhere. You search in vain for the other driver, then realize that there *is* no other driver because the car you hit was parked.

What do you do? Before rushing into an ill-considered course of action, a responsible driver should ask several important questions:

A) Did anyone see you?
(If the answer is "no," skip directly to Step 2)

B) Is the car you hit an expensive car?
(If "yes" go back and make damn sure you answered Question A correctly.)

C) Is there any chance you can pin this on them?
(It's a parked car. So probably not.)

D) Teenagers only: How long will you be grounded if your parents find out?
(If "a long time," double-check Question A again.)

E) Have you done something positive for the world recently which could counterbalance a brief lapse in moral judgment?
(If "no" proceed to Question F. Or go back to Question A)

F) Could you do something positive for the world tomorrow which could counterbalance a brief lapse in moral judgment today?
(If "no" proceed to Step 1, but you're not being very imaginative.)

Responsible Steps to Take After Hitting a Parked Car and Answering Above Questions

Step 1. Write a note to leave on the windshield of the car you hit containing your name, license number, insurance provider and all relevant contact information.

But wait! There is a Good Way and a Bad Way to write this note:

Bad Way to Leave Note

Hi. My name is Lisa Robertson. Sorry, I think I bumped your car. My license number is FL3768912, my insurance carrier is Reliable Insurance, policy #AF692774561209D, my telephone number is 458-1295. I will take full financial responsibility for any damage I may have caused.

Sincerely, Lisa Robertson

Good Way to Leave Note

hi my name is ~~Robertson~~ Sorry,
i think i bumped your car my
license number is ~~FL3~~ my insurance
carrier is ~~Reliable~~ insurance policy
~~AF692~~ my telephone
number is 458. i will take full
financial responsibility
for any damage i may have caused
sincerely, ~~Robertson~~

Step 2. Drive away

Summary

Handwriting is also a good way to add a personal touch to an amusing chapter summary which is somewhat lacking in the amusing part. For example:

A rabbi hits a parked car ~~[illegible]~~ turns to the ~~[illegible]~~ who ~~[illegible]~~ then the priest says, ~~[illegible]~~ with a car like that. ~~[illegible]~~ so the bartender jumps in the back seat! ~~[illegible several lines]~~ not in my hot air balloon!

U-Turn

Good Things About Being a Bad Driver

1. No matter how late you are, no matter how slow traffic is going, as long as you can go faster and stay ahead of the guy next to you, you win!

2. Lack of concern for the law and other drivers' safety can significantly reduce travel time.

3. Passengers in your vehicle have low performance expectations which are easy to exceed.

4. Endless opportunities to take revenge on the world for the many insults you have suffered in a safe, controlled environment.

5. The people you really care about will be spared when you take your anger out on perfect strangers.

6. Friends will never ask you to drive them anywhere.

7. Get to know your local law enforcement officers.

CHAPTER 14

Freeway Driving: No Lights, No Intersections, No Problem

Since on your side of the freeway everyone is traveling in the same direction (theoretically) and there is no cross traffic (you hope), the only form of entertainment available is changing lanes.

Defending Your Lane

The relationship between a bad driver and her lane is best imagined as like that of a mother bear and her cubs: affectionate, nurturing, and *very* protective. When you see a turn signal flashing on the car in the lane next to yours, you must determine how to deal with this potential threat. There are several options, including:

1) Safely accelerate to let this person in behind you.
2) Drive at the same speed as this person, accelerating and decelerating in pace to ensure the lane change can never be made.

These are the main choices, although there may be others— honking your horn is always good. If your opponent somehow manages to pull off the lane change, sneaking in without your knowing, it is your responsibility to change lanes also, pass the offending driver, and glance over with contempt.

With this in mind, if it is *you* making the lane change, give the person in the next lane as little chance as possible to block you from changing lanes. Signaling is clearly out.

Another approach is the Passenger-Assisted Lane Squeeze:

1. Make eye contact.
2. Make pleading, apologetic request for admittance into lane.
3. Establish bond of brotherhood and understanding between yourself and potential yielder, expressing your tender, human side.
4. Enter lane, yell "Sucker!"
5. Accelerate.

Defending Your Freeway

A related topic is your responsibility, as a driver in the right-hand lane, to defend your freeway against outsiders trying to muscle in from the merging lane to your right. Is there really any more room for another vehicle? If, as is likely, you determine there are already too many other drivers on the freeway, you must seal off the border.

Entertaining Your Passengers on a Freeway

When telling a story while traveling at 85 miles per hour, it's essential to establish and maintain eye contact with each and every passenger, especially those in the back seat, who might otherwise feel left out. Passengers will pay greater attention, be more engaged in your story, and be grateful that you are including them. Also, hand gestures to emphasize dramatic moments are strongly recommended. Storytelling is a performance, and your car a theater. If you pay too much attention to the road, (which really isn't necessary because there are no traffic lights or stop signs), your passengers will see you as disengaged, and before you know it they'll stop listening and begin talking among themselves. It is you who will be left out of the conversation, becoming a mere chauffeur.

Freeway Signs You Don't Want to See

Safety Tip for Teenagers

The fundamental question you must answer about freeway driving is: *How fast can your parents' minivan really go?* Make sure you know the maximum speed. Often we assume that sports cars are faster. That is not necessarily so. In any case, it is essential that you know the maximum speed in the event that a hypothetical situation in which you must travel at that maximum speed as a safety precaution, should occur.

Summary

Does having multiple personality disorder qualify us to drive in the car pool lane?

CHAPTER 15

Dealing with Cops: Remember, They Love a Good Chase

We all know from watching years of standup comedy that getting pulled over is often a hilarious situation, a great source of comedic inspiration. So when you get pulled over, pay attention, because funny things are bound to be happening left and right. You don't want to miss out on the chance to tell a great story.

Cops look forward to these comedic moments just as much as standup comedians and regular people, so play your part: wait until the officer has reached your window, then as a joke, *reach for the glove box quickly!* If the officer then grabs for his gun, you say, "Gotcha!" Now he's in a good mood, and ready for some more humorous banter. Try:

"I intended to obey the speed limit, but my speedometer doesn't seem to be working. Either that, or I'm just too drunk to read the numbers."

If the officer starts off with the classic, "Do you know why I pulled you over?" be prepared with some snappy comebacks:

"I'll bet you're going to tell me." Or:

"Because you're an a**hole?" Or:

"Give me a few choices, I'm sure I'll get it." Or:

"You don't know, either?"

Other Ways to Start a Conversation with the Officer Who Has Pulled You Over

→ Cops are lazy. If the officer has to walk all the way to your car, the battle is already lost. Meet him half way at the very least, better yet, go directly to the patrol car so the cop doesn't have to get out of his vehicle at all. Then try:

"Do you know who I *am*?!" (Say you're a relative of some famous or important person. Cops are very impressed by this.) or:

"I know you don't get paid much: here's ten bucks, go buy your wife a nice dress."

→ Of course some cops are women. If you're lucky enough to get one of these, be sure and let her know how tickled you are to be pulled over by a woman cop. Whatever she says, keep coming back to the novelty value of her being both a cop and a woman.

→ If you're answering all the questions, the officer is in control. Take control of the conversation by starting with:

"First, I'll need your name and badge number. And your supervising officer."

If the Issue is Speed

→ Cops are just like any other people—they are open to persuasion. A good point to make is that you're a *lot* more alert at 95 than you are at 55. Speeding is a well known way to combat dangerous driver fatigue.

→ Getting out of a ticket is all about your presentation skills and your ability to reason with police officers. It's a good idea to practice this technique in case of an unfortunate, actual occasion when you need to use it. So upon getting your license, it's always a good idea to speed through a few speed traps, get pulled over and practice your negotiation skills in preparation for the actual event. Then explain to the officer you were just practicing, not really speeding.

Summary for Good Drivers

You didn't have to read this chapter because you'll never get pulled over, because your driving is such a f**king inspiration for the rest of us.

Summary for Cops

Do you want to know why so many people hate you? It's your all-stick-no-carrot attitude. Where's the *positive* reinforcement? The pat on the back for a safe-driving technique? The block of cheese at the end of the maze? Start giving out lollipops for drivers who drive within posted speed limits, and you'll start seeing some real changes. They'll still hate you, but for other reasons.

Summary for Bad Drivers

If you're unable to resist the temptation to speed, make illegal turns, tailgate and drive with reckless disregard for the safety of everyone else on the road, you probably *are* a cop.

How To Tell Your Neighbors You Just Ran Over Their Dog

Tell them there are lots of better dogs available.

Remind them that it's just a stupid dog. Not like a kid or something.

Let them know it wasn't good for your tires, either.

Remind them they don't have to pay for dog food anymore.

Blame your kids.

Tell them you're already starting to feel better about it, and they probably will soon as well.

Let them down gently: "You know that dog you used to have . . . ?"

CHAPTER 16

Parking: Your Opportunity to Contribute to the Financial Well-Being of Your City

Whose Parking Spot Is It, Anyway?

Test your Parking Intelligence Quotient (PIQ):

This spot properly belongs to:

A) The car in front of the spot.
B) The car behind the spot.
C) The car which arrived there first.
D) The larger car with the more violent-appearing driver.
E) You, no matter where you are or when you got there.

If you answered anything other than E), there's nothing we can do for you. Your brain has been taken over by the DMV and its foreign allies, and you are no longer capable of independent action. Hesitation in this situation will allow people to steal parking places which are rightfully yours faster than you can say, "I'm a baguette-eating French Communist."

Many parking spaces were designed for smaller, less important cars than the one you drive. To secure the necessary room for your larger, better car, you must use the advanced technique known as VIP Parking:

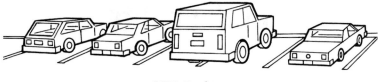

VIP Parking

Backing Up

An essential part of parking is backing up. Here's how to do it right:

Step 1. Check mirrors.
Step 2. Check carefully behind by looking over your shoulder.
Step 3. Still looking directly behind you, step on the gas.
Step 4. You *are* in reverse, right?
Step 5. Ooops. Looks like you forgot about Step 4.
Step 6. Leave a note. (See Chapter 13)

Did You Know: If you get boxed in by other, smaller cars in a parking space, you have a legal right to smash into them, and bash your way free.

Vocabulary Alert

A "Parking Brake" is that thing you put on when you park on a hill, then forget to take off, so that when you drive, you grind up very important stuff on your car, inflicting irreparable damage.

Proper Exiting Technique for Head-in Parking Lots

Sometimes it's the little things in driving that leave the biggest impressions.

Incorrect Method   **Correct Method**

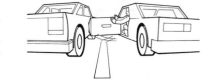

Parking Signs

It is the job of your local Parking Authority to place clearly marked "No Parking" signs on your city streets which are so confusing you can't possibly determine when or if it's OK to park. This guarantees that your government will continue to function, since it is entirely dependent on parking fines for the revenue needed to invent and post the confusing signs and pay the parking enforcement officers to write the resulting parking tickets.

Effective Parking Sign   Ineffective Parking Sign

**2 Hr Parking 9 AM—5 AM,
Monday—Wednesday**
Zone 3 Permits Exempt on
Tuesday, Except for the ones
with the blue sticker on the
left corner
No Parking Every 6th Day, for
example, if there's No Parking
on Wednesday of this week, next
week there will be No Parking
on Tuesday, and so on. No
Stopping Anytime for cars with
cargo weight rating above or
below 140 kg
Except Sunday

**No
Parking
Anytime**

Summary

If you park on an upward hill facing downward, always angle your wheels away from the curb by turning the steering wheel counterclockwise in the northern hemisphere (if you're on the east side of the street). If you're on the west side of the street pointing uphill on the downhill side, and you've crossed the equator where the toilets flush in the opposite direction, the reverse is true. Except on Wednesdays (Zone 3 Permits exempt).

U-Turn

The Handicapped Parking Question

The Handicapped Parking question is, simply put: Aren't we all, in some way handicapped? The answer: Of course we are! There's the obvious physical handicap, and the less obvious mental handicap. When you come to think of it, most of your best friends are probably mentally handicapped, at least about certain subjects, like their taste in music. And then there is the emotional handicap. Not the chronic or permanent variety, but rather the occasional, temporary emotional handicap brought on by stress, for example, the stress of not being able to find a parking space.

What could be more stressful than arriving at a parking lot in front of a medical building when you're late for a doctor's appointment and being unable to park in the most convenient spot? It is especially stressful when you see, right in front of the entrance, an empty handicapped parking space! Clearly there isn't the time to apply for a temporary emotionally handicapped sticker. So you must self-diagnose. Ask yourself these questions:

1. Am I very late?
2. Has this made me agitated and upset?
3. Has my agitation been aggravated by the spectacle of the empty handicapped parking space which nobody is using?
4. Do I have anything to hang on my mirror which looks like it might be a handicapped parking permit, but which can be placed in such a way that it can't be read, maybe with an article of clothing accidentally slung over it?

If you can honestly answer "yes" to these questions, you are suffering from a temporary emotional disability, and should definitely park in the handicapped parking space.

CHAPTER 17

Traffic Jams: More Fun Than Major Surgery, Less Fun Than Minor Surgery

Our country is divided by race, class, age, gender, ethnic background, region, politics and religion. But there is one thing which unites us: we share the road, where we are all equal. The ancient VW Beetle still has the right of way over the newly purchased Lexus if the Beetle arrives first at the four-way STOP sign. Especially if the Beetle doesn't stop.

While we are all equal on the road, nowhere are we more equal than in a traffic jam. Traffic jams are the Great Equalizers. While love of mankind and unity of purpose may not be your first reaction to being stuck in gridlock, as you look out at your brothers and sisters stranded and miserable just like you, you realize we're all inching along together in the traffic jam of life. You look to your left and there's a beat-up, 20-year-old Honda Civic driven by a possibly undocumented worker. You look to your right and there is a white stretch limo, just as stuck as you and the undocumented worker. While you can't see inside because of the tinted windows, you can be sure that whoever's inside is frustrated by the traffic just like you. Well, maybe not *as* frustrated, submerged in an interior Jacuzzi sipping champagne and sampling various hors d'oeuvres, but frustrated nonetheless.

So as you can see we're all one, united by traffic jams. Except for Bill Gates, who is flying overhead in his own private plane. And all his rich friends. And the a**holes in the carpool lane. And that jerk zipping ahead between lanes on his motorcycle.

Other Good Things About Traffic Jams

1. You can burn up a few of those required hours teaching your youngster how to drive in a major traffic jam. There's nothing safer than traveling 5 to 10 m.p.h. on a freeway from 4:00 to 7:00 P.M. on a weekday.

2. You can examine in detail every little bit of the highway you previously flew by without giving it a second thought.

3. Feel like you're a newsmaker when you hear about the jam you're in on the radio.

4. Good exercise for hard-to-target small muscles in your ankle as you switch back and forth from accelerator to brake.

Summary

Stuck in traffic, and not going anywhere? Try honking. If that doesn't work, honk louder.

PAGE 96

Thank you for visiting page 96, the "General Information Window," a subsection of "**Chapter 8, Making Your Visit to the DMV Successful.**" There will be a one hour wait while the agent at the General Information Window takes a 10-minute coffee break.

If you have waited for an hour, wait another 15 minutes.

OK, it's your turn now. What do you want? You want to sell your car? Take this green ticket with the number 2158, and go to the "Documentation Verification Window," which is located on page 130.

Please go now to page 130. Thank you.

CHAPTER 18

Off-Roading: Fun for You, Good for Your Car, Great for the National Wildlife Refuge

EXTERIOR: THE COLORADO ROCKIES—SUNRISE

A family of deer laps the dew off a berry bush on a high peak towering over a leafy gorge. A spotted owl hoots in the distance, a rainbow trout leaps out of a rippling brook beneath a cascading waterfall to snare a dragonfly. A brown bear bounds out of his cave in search of sustenance for the long winter ahead. The early bud of a rare mountain cactus flower stretches towards the sun's rays like a young bird, as rose-colored clouds sweep across the azure sky.

What is missing from this picture?

That's easy! A big, carbon-monoxide spewing, 4,000 pound SUV.

But wait, here comes two of them, racing along the creek bed, kicking rocks and splashing mud into the camera lens as they barrel along the intricate ecosystem of the valley floor, tires ripping into the delicate new growth of the mountainside! What manly fun! This could be you! A new you. A kind of you that's always been there, but was hiding in the back of your sensible, high mileage 4 cylinder Camry. This could be your new car. (And the wife will love it, because it's safe for the kids!)

CUT TO:

INTERIOR: CLEAN SUV—TWO YEARS LATER, PACKED WITH GROCERIES

So you wussed out. You bought a $28,000 SUV with four wheel drive because you thought it would turn you into a Mountain Man and send you on amazing adventures in the wilderness, but instead, you just basically drove it around the same streets you used to drive on with your Camry. That's all right. You did buy the car, which must somehow reflect an untamed, rugged, animal-of-the-earth personality that is inside you somewhere. You don't actually have to do all that stuff in the commercials. Drive out somewhere where you can see a tree, put a bunch of mud all over your car, and call it a day. After all, it gets kind of lonely out there with no one to cut off, tailgate, verbally harass and endanger.

Summary

Sadly, there are still some areas of our beautiful land inaccessible to cars. But recent appointees to the U.S. Forest Service, the Department of the Interior and the Environmental Protection Agency are all working to correct this problem. Soon there will be total automobile access. In the meantime, these appointees are keeping busy by nurturing their friendships with top executives at various mining, logging and energy companies, inventing personal income tax loopholes for those friends, and kicking squirrels.

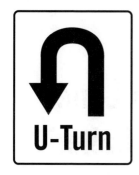

U-Turn

Exercises You Can Do While Driving

Like black-and-white movies, record players and classical music, exercise no longer serves a legitimate purpose in modern society. While the widespread availability of automobiles has made traditional exercise completely unnecessary, some insist on these primitive activities out of ignorance, fear and superstition. According to the health nut/car-hater crowd, the only way to get a healthy workout requires that you get out of your car, hike in the mountains, bicycle or kayak through wilderness areas, things which people who have no jobs and are useless to society have plenty of time to do. But in fact a fitness program designed for a behind-the-wheel lifestyle can be more effective than the non-vehicular-based system, and you can do it all while driving.

Safety Tip

When exercising while driving when other cars are present on the road, it's of *utmost* importance to stay hydrated and stretch all relevant muscle groups before *and* after workouts.

→ Get your heart rate aerobic by closing your eyes while driving, especially on the freeway.

→ Bounce up and down on your seat.

→ Strength training: tow heavy objects.

→ Roll windows up and down five sets of 20 (electric windows: more reps may be necessary)

→ Sweat off excess calories in your own private car sauna by rolling up windows, turning heat up to maximum on a hot summer day.

→ Seat Back Sit-ups: release seat back lever, push all the way back, thrust forward, repeat.

CHAPTER 19

Underutilized Lanes (Sometimes Called "Sidewalks")

With state and local revenues for road-building squeezed by competing needs like revising high school science textbooks to eliminate references to controversial, unproven theories like evolution, it is more important than ever to develop cost-effective ways to ease congestion on our city streets and highways.

Here is where you, the bad driver, can make an important contribution to your state, your city, county and even your local neighborhood. You can save the taxpayers millions of dollars by personally expanding a road or freeway, adding an extra lane without the enormous expense of road-building and years of construction tie-ups.

For example, let's consider the "sidewalk." This wasteful big-government-bureaucracy spending boondoggle has outlived its usefulness, if it ever had any. It is a remnant of a failed policy which has created a culture of dependency, encouraging pedestrians to gather and loiter in an artificially protected area, which should rightfully belong to drivers. Through the soft bigotry of low expectations, the government removes from pedestrians the crucial incentive to rise up from the never-ending cycle of pedestrianism to better their lives.

It is therefore better for you and better for them if you remove this unearned entitlement by driving onto the so-called "sidewalk."

Safety Alert

→ It is not good for your car to drive on a sidewalk which is more than moderately crowded with pedestrians.

Eventually we need to get back these occupied territories which, incidentally, used to be called "sidelanes." Although it is standard policy never to negotiate with pedestrians, all options (yes, including diplomacy) are on the table.

Other Underutilized Lanes

Traffic signs, especially on freeways, are necessarily short because you're driving at a safe speed consistent with "the flow of traffic" (about 85 m.p.h.) and you don't have a lot of time to read long-winded road signs. However, in their zeal to make these signs as short as possible, sometimes highway engineers shorten them too much. The unabridged, original message of the "Exit Only Lane" is actually: "Exit Only If You're Not Already Using This Lane as a Passing or Driving Lane." Most drivers don't realize this, and as a result they are reluctant to fully use the Exit Lane in all of it's many functions.

Another underutilized lane is "the shoulder." This is a wonderful, extra lane you can use to relieve pressure on the other lanes when they are congested, thus aiding the free flow of traffic. Unfortunately, inconsiderate drivers, especially inconsiderate drivers whose cars have broken down, sometimes use this lane to park. This complicates things for you when you're using the lane as a driving lane.

Another lane which isn't doing a hell of a lot except taking up space is that one in the middle of a two-way street marked with two lines, an inner broken line, and an outer solid line. This lane, technically referred to as The Big Empty Space in the Middle of the Road Lane, clearly can be used for passing.

Chapter Summary

Pedestrians and recovering pedestrians can look forward to a day when alternatives to walking are more available to everybody. One of many "tough love" initiatives, the No Pedestrian Left Behind Bill which will eliminate all sidewalks, has already passed the House and needs just a few more votes to pass in the Senate.

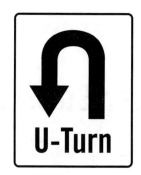

Road Signs You Can Ignore

Any sign posted inside a building, like a parking garage, purporting to tell you which way you can turn exiting the building, is put there by the building owners, and is *not a real road sign.* You can ignore it completely. It may look like a real road sign, but that's just to try and fool you.

You've already paid the bandits and their agents in the little booth near the exit a fat ransom to escape the captivity your car has been held in. It's certainly none of their business where you go after paying the ransom. If the cleverly-designed-to-look-like-a-road-sign message said, "Do Exactly What Your Wife Tells You to Do," or "Do Not Break Up with Your Boyfriend," would you follow their instructions? Of course you wouldn't. You may treat their "Right Turn Only" signs with the same disregard.

This is also true for fake road signs posted in the driveways of drive-through fast-food restaurants and other businesses you may be leaving. Are you going to let Ronald McDonald tell you how to drive?

CHAPTER 20

Coping with Driver Stress: Yoga, Meditation, and Verbally Abusing Other Drivers

Let's face it: we live in a stressful world. That's why so many have turned to yoga and meditation to find inner peace. By putting aside the stress and tumult of our everyday lives, it's possible to reconnect with the peaceful place at the center of your chakra, or whatever it is that your peaceful place is at the center of. But it's difficult, is it not, to find inner peace when you're LATE FOR YOUR GODDAMN YOGA CLASS!

And why are you late? You're late because of the a**hole in the Mercedes who's taking up TWO LANES and doesn't know where the f**king hell he's going! All that stands between you and serenity is this idiot who doesn't know how to drive. Your pranayama energy is losing more and more of its transcendental luminescence with every passing moment. You know your yoga power is only supposed to be used for good, but you're about two seconds away from strangling this jerk with your yoga mat. And maybe if this woman who is stopped at the light would look up from putting on her makeup she'd see the LIGHT HAS TURNED GREEN. You can GO now, lady!

These meat-eating, unfit, unhealthy, spiritually backwards slobs should be ground up and fed to the cows they eat for food. You're way behind schedule now, and your yoga instructor gets so mad when you're late. Your inner peace has been totally compromised. You're barely going to have time for stretching and breathing—you'll be lucky to get five minutes of meditation, and then you'll have to go back on the road with these cretins.

On the other hand, since you're probably going to miss meditation, and possibly the entire class, maybe a few verbal outbursts can substitute for the consciousness-raising, healing power of yoga. By rolling down your window and telling these s.o.b.s exactly what you think of their driving, you can achieve relaxation, rejuvenation and relief. Visualize yourself cursing out another driver and then speeding away while he chokes on your exhaust. An increased sense of calmness and peace settles over you like a gentle cloud. You feel lighter. Your body has been rid of toxins. Your aura has a vibrant, radiant glow. You are now fully connected to your own true nature, experiencing a heightened sense of the interconnectedness of all living things. Except for that living thing in the Lincoln Continental who just cut you off. Switch lanes immediately, draw alongside him, yell something unprintable, give him the finger and cut him off right back! This provides you with something traditional western medicine can't give you. The wounded self is now whole.

Summary

The cathartic, liberating tranquility achievable through bad driving is another example of the numerous positive aspects of bad driving you won't hear about from the bra-burning radicals of the mainstream press. This is just one more thing Dan Rather doesn't want you to know about.

CHAPTER 21

Maps and Other Insults to Your Natural Sense of Direction

There are two kinds of maps. The most common is the kind you can pick up at gas stations, which are *way* too small to read. You can use this kind of map if you're willing to pull over to the side of the road, take out a magnifying glass, and if it's dark, a flashlight and study it at length. If you do all of this, you still won't be able to read the map, because it's still way too small. Also, pulling over to the side of the road to read a map is the ultimate sign of defeat, and reflects poorly on your strength of character. A good bad driver can be blindfolded and spun around 15 times, and when asked to point north, still can point confidently in some direction.

The other kind of map is the expensive, book-like encyclopedia-sized map, like the *Thomas Brothers Guide*, which is entirely readable because each page covers an area of approximately a block and a half. If you want to follow the street you're on for more than a block and a half, you have to turn to another page, which is in a completely different part of the book. Then, if the street should happen to turn a little, you have to go to another page in another different section of the book, or more likely another book. But you can read the names of the streets, and also the numbers. So basically, if you're lost, at least you'll be able to find out a lot of information about the street you're lost on, although you won't be able to find out where that street is in relation to where you want to go, or in relation to anything else.

So there's really no point in trying to use a map. A better solution is simply never to admit you are lost. "Lost" is not a word in the bad driver's vocabulary, except when explaining, "No, we're not lost!"

Asking for directions from a passerby or another driver is even worse. It puts your ignorance and weakness on display. It's like asking for help opening a jar. If you're not strong enough to open it, you don't deserve what's inside.

If you're uncertain about where you're going, keep driving. Eventually, you'll get there. And do *not* slow down to look for street signs or numbers. There's nothing more aggravating than driving behind someone who's slowing down because they're lost. If you're not where you want to be when you want to be there, the obvious solution is to drive *faster*, not slower.

Calling 411 Driving Directions

If you're a complete failure as a human being and insist on getting help, at least get help from an anonymous, faceless bureaucracy like 411 Driving Directions so nobody will know. This is a really cool service that comes with your cell phone. Noting that they charge by the second, a wise driver will attempt to minimize the amount of time spent on these conversations. Your conversation will go something like this:

THEM
Hello, and thank you——

YOU
Yeah—I need directions from——

THEM

—thank you for calling 411 Driver Direction Serv—

YOU

I'm on Sunset heading to the Valley. I need directions to—

THEM

—*Services*, accessing multiple media data bases—

YOU

OK, OK. Just tell me how to get to—

THEM

—to better assist you in whatever way we can, to get you where you need to be going quickly.

YOU

. . . Are you done yet?

THEM

This service is brought to you by a conglomeration of various phone companies—

YOU

Look, I just need f**king directions from—

THEM

—map makers, state governments, and foreign intelligence agencies. My name is Pierre. How may I help you?

YOU

Aw, forget it.

THEM
Thank you for calling 411 Driving Directions
services. A charge of $49.95 will be posted to
your phone bill.

Fortunately, due to the advanced technology of GPS guidance systems, you don't have to talk to an annoying human
being anymore, you can talk to your car. But you don't want
your car to think you're an idiot, so play it cool:

YOU
Just double checking those directions . . .

YOUR CAR
Turn left at the corner.

YOU
I knew that!

YOUR CAR
Of course you did. You're a human and I'm
just a stupid car.

YOU
Are you making fun of me?

YOUR CAR
No. You're a real genius. Honest.

YOU
That's it. No oil change for you.

YOUR CAR
Ah, go f**k yourself.

Internet Directions

Today, you don't have to mess with maps or 411 or GPS. All you have to do is type your starting point and destination into an Internet map search site to receive surprisingly accurate driving directions such as the following:

1. Go north on Braddock Ave	.5 mi	2 min
2. Left onto Oak Blvd	2.8 mi	6 min
3. Take wrong turn onto Culver	3 mi	8 min
4. Realize you're going wrong way, turn around	4 mi	10 min
5. Still can't find 28th St., start getting angry about low quality of directions you got on the Internet	3.4 mi	9 min
6. Continue on Culver southbound, still looking for 28th street, driving faster to make up for lost time	7.6 mi	8 min
7. F**king stupid computer program gave me sh**ty directions, Godf**king damnit!!	5.3 mi	2 min
8. Get pulled over on 28th street, ironically enough	2.2 mi	1 min
9. Lose argument with police officer, transfer to back of squad car, turn west on Robertson	6.7 mi	10 min
10. Arrive at Police Headquarters, get booked	5.1 mi	8 min

Total trip 40.6 mi 1 hr 6 min (approx.)

Giving Directions

People who are from around where you live know where they're going and don't need any directions. It's only outsiders, from some other place, who probably don't have any business driving around your neighborhood, who will stop you to ask directions. Here's how to help them:

> YOU
>
> You want to get to highway 54 going north? No problem. You go straight down this road you're on past the corner where the tractor shop used to be before they moved over to Booneville after the factory closed the first time, in '78. Same year the football team came in second in the state. Would've won the championship too, if the Baxter boy hadn't dropped that pass in the end zone. Whole family had to move after that. Don't suppose we'll be seein' them for a while. But don't take the new road. Go past the old graveyard road, and bear right after you pass the Harris place—they're not there now, it's rented out to the summer people. Nice folks. The kid's a little strange though. I tell you, there's something wrong with that boy. They say he goes out to the Old Pond at night and howls at the moon, they say. Shouldn't bother you, though. Long's you don't look him in the eye.

Summary

Some men feel comfortable asking for directions every now and then, without feeling that it calls into question their masculinity. For example, if they get lost on the way to the ballet, they are not ashamed to ask for help.

CHAPTER 22

Car Maintenance: Ten Things Which Sound Important Need to Be Fixed Right Now

Every once in a while you need to get your oil changed. Sometimes dealerships offer this service at a huge discount, or even for free. You take advantage of this great offer, and it's good that you do, because there are 10 things you've never heard of that need to be fixed! Luckily the mechanics who check out your car discover these things just in time. By taking care of them now, you'll be sure your car won't explode. And it's only going to cost you $1,480.63.

But the oil change is free.

Here's the rundown of necessary repairs you need to attend to right away ranging in urgency from critical to dire.

Crucial Part — Necessary Maintenance

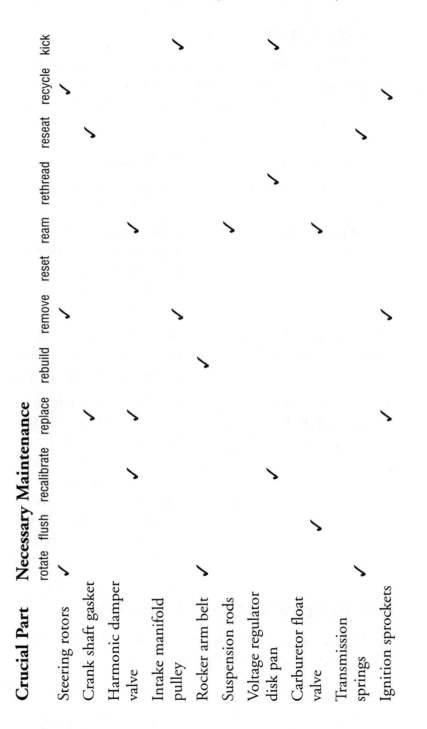

Crucial Part	rotate	flush	recalibrate	replace	rebuild	remove	reset	ream	rethread	reseat	recycle	kick
Steering rotors	✓										✓	
Crank shaft gasket				✓						✓		
Harmonic damper valve			✓	✓				✓				
Intake manifold pulley						✓						✓
Rocker arm belt		✓			✓							
Suspension rods								✓				
Voltage regulator disk pan			✓					✓	✓			✓
Carburetor float valve				✓		✓						
Transmission springs	✓									✓		
Ignition sprockets											✓	

Mechanics' Jargon: A Glossary

To be an informed consumer you must be able to speak the language of your car maintenance professional. Some repairs may sound confusing, but involve basic principles that anyone can understand.

If Your Mechanic Says	He Means
Your intake manifold pulley needs to be rebuilt.	I lost a bet last night, and I'm a bit low on cash.
Your voltage regulator disk needs to be rotated.	After doing a lot of diagnostic testing, it became apparent that the insurance company won't pay for my wife's cosmetic surgery.
Your carburetor float valve needs to be flushed.	Something expensive in your car is definitely broken. I know because I broke it.
It's just a loose screw in the ignition system.	In order to tighten it I'll have to remove and dismantle every other part of your car's engine, transmission, exhaust, cooling and electrical systems, which will all turn out to be defective and need to be replaced.

Self-Diagnosis: What These Noises Mean

You can train your ear to identify problems before, or at least as they become extremely expensive.

When You Hear	It Means
Tink, tink tink.	Your car is about to explode.
Clacka-clacka-clacka.	Your car is hungry, not just for food, but for adventure and fulfilment.
Hsssssssssssss.	With any luck it's only a highly poisonous snake coiled around the brake pedal.
Choo, choo.	Your car is struggling with identity issues.
Ramalamadingdong.	Somebody put a ram in your ramalamadingdong and it must be removed.
Shoudoup, shoubeedo.	Something went terribly wrong with your engine in the still of last night.
Yjka;j4907542gq9bn90uqriha2h53.	Your car is typing randomly.
BOOM! BOOM! BOOM!	The guy in your trunk is not dead yet.

Common Problems You Can Fix Yourself

→ If you hear a funny noise coming from the engine compartment that sounds like a kind of a clickita-clackita-clickita, and it gets louder and faster as you accelerate, turn your radio up until you can no longer hear it.

→ If you detect a mixture of oil and water underneath your car, this could mean a possible crack in your engine block. Before this becomes a major problem, sell the car.

→ If you smell gasoline in the passenger compartment when you step on the accelerator, which usually indicates a leak in the fuel line, go immediately to an auto parts store and buy several Pine Forest Wild Cherry Country Orchid Double Mocha Fudge Scented Tree-Shaped Cardboard Air Fresheners.

→ If you determine that an oil leak is traceable to a busted head gasket, don't overlook the power of positive thinking. Send your car love energy at regular intervals throughout the day. Visualize the healing process.

Summary

And don't forget to get your oil changed every 50,000 miles.

CHAPTER 23

Insurance: You're Paying for It, You Might As Well Use It

Vocabulary Alert

Insurance — A system in which you pay a monthly fee so that if you get into an accident, you can do everything in your power to make sure your insurance company doesn't find out. This ensures that you pay for the repairs, not the insurance company. No one actually knows what insurance is good for. Some speculate that it provides an "on the brighter side" sort of comfort when you get into an accident and can say, "Unfortunately, I had an accident today, but at least my insurance company doesn't know."

In the old days, when cars were made of heavy, awkward materials like steel and were equipped with front and rear bumpers all mounted at the same, dull height from the ground, cars could collide with each other at slow speeds with little or no damage. These mishaps were known as "fender benders" and could be dismissed as too insignificant to repair.

Today, due to advanced automobile design, cars are made with modern, lightweight materials, like origami paper, and every car on the road is protected by bumpers mounted at different, individually unique heights.

This guarantees *maximum possible damage,* or in the lingo of body shop workers, "mpd," to distinguish it from *minimum possible damage.* (Also known as "mpd" since they are identical.)

As a result of these innovations, major damage can occur if you stare with any degree of intensity at the rear end of another car, for a period of five or more seconds. Any more than that will cause them to collapse. If in addition to staring, you actually touch another car with yours, the bumpers will implode entirely in what is known as a breakaway safety precaution, because a car which collapses in an accident like an egg shell is clearly safer.

Fortunately, no matter what damage you do to your car and/or the one you've hit, there are body shops waiting to help. Body shops are equipped with sophisticated repair tools including drilling equipment, various pullers and benders, hammers, sanders, patching compounds and computer-aided paint matching systems. The repair specialist will carefully assess the damage to you car, and then after a complex analysis will announce, "Oh, that can't be repaired, it has to be replaced."

Turns out the complicated repair equipment is part of a mandatory museum display area that all body shops are required to carry. Ask when the next tour is and you can be escorted through this area by a competent guide who will explain the history of body shops and how this "repair" equipment was used in the old days.

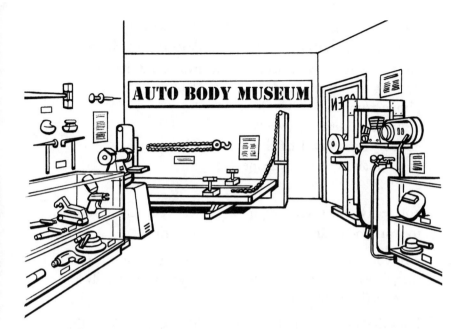

The good news about replacement parts is that they are not only "like new," they are *in fact* new. The bad news is that whatever part of the car must be replaced, it will cost approximately 80% of the cost of the car. But then, you're insured, so after a deductible of only a few thousand dollars, you're covered, which means the insurance company will pay for the damage, then raise your rates to the level (approximately) of the national debt.

Even though they're not much help when you get into accidents, at least you know when you get into other kinds of sticky, costly situations like moving traffic violations, they will also not be helpful.

Good Things About Accidents

Great way to meet someone. You get their name, address, phone number, plus you have a shared experience to talk about right away. Isn't that better than meeting someone at a bar?

You really didn't want to go to work today, anyway.

Test your air bags to make sure they're packed correctly for effective deployment.

If it's the other driver's fault, you can get repairs you should have taken care of months ago done on the other person's dime.

Bad Things About Accidents

Ever heard the phrase, "bad omen"?

Yeah, but you just totaled your *car*.

Air bags must be repacked, so you'll never really know.

It's just a car. Your life is still a jumble of ignored responsibilities, ditched ambitions and cowardly compromises.

Summary

While it's expensive, your automobile insurance policy enables you to sleep well at night, knowing that whatever catastrophes may come your way, those monthly premiums will provide protection and security for the insurance company executives and their lawyers.

U-Turn

The Many Different Shades of "Stop"

It is said that Eskimos have 50 different words for "snow." Bad drivers have 50 different words for "stop." Here is a non-exhaustive list of some of the many stops which are available to you at any given STOP sign.

The Standard Stop—Altered state of awareness resulting from visual contact with stop sign and possible mental engagement with the concept of stopping.

The Full Stop—A barely detectable or theoretical slowing induced by momentarily taking foot off the accelerator and waving it briefly over the brake pedal.

The Complete Stop—Pressure is not only retracted from the accelerator, it is also applied to the brake by actual, physical contact with the foot. It is accompanied by a brief glance in at least one direction of cross traffic.

The Complete and Total Stop—Significant decrease in velocity accompanied by a thorough examination of cross traffic from both directions.

The "All Way" Stop—Some stops signs have a note at the bottom: "All Way" which, taken literally, means "stop all the way," or "bring your vehicle to a state of *suspended motion,* much like parking, where your wheels *temporarily cease all forward movement.*" If this note is not present, you should use one of the previous stops.

The DMV Driving Test Stop—This is the stop you do when taking your road test for your driver's license. It can be defined as: An "All Way" Stop *behind* the white line for at least three seconds.

The You-Must-Not-Be-From-Around-Here Stop—Similar to the DMV Driving Test Stop except that there is no driving examiner present. *Caution:* Extremely dangerous maneuver.

Advanced Techniques

CHAPTER 24

Back-Seat Driving: Drivers Want Your Advice, They're Just Too Shy to Ask

Given your outstanding driving ability, you should always be the one doing the driving, but in some cases, like when your license has been revoked, you may find yourself assuming the under-appreciated role of the back-seat driver.

(Note: to be an effective back-seat driver you don't actually have to *be* in the back seat. Some of the finest back-seat driving is done from the front passenger seat. However, advice given from the back seat is doubly annoying and insulting to the driver, so it's really the preferred location.)

For the most part, there are few resources at your disposal for learning the techniques required for this important skill, not to mention the fact that it is completely ignored by the freedom-hating vegetarians responsible for *The DMV Driver's Handbook*.

Basic Techniques

Always State the Obvious. You can never be too sure that a driver has noticed any of the other cars on the road, or is anticipating what they're likely to do. "Watch out for that car turning left ahead," is a typical piece of back-seat driving. By itself it may not be too annoying, but together with similar alarms about every other car and what's happening on the road, it's like piling the straws one by one on the camel's back. The driver will ignore you most of the time until one day he will explode in a volcanic eruption of pent-up rage, to which you respond innocently, "All I said was there's a car turning left. Just trying to help."

Help Driver Maintain Satisfactory Driving Speed. If the driver is being passed by other cars, he probably is unaware of the speed limit. Drivers appreciate a verbal reminder of what that is. If you want to be more subtle, ask if there's something wrong with the car. If, on the other hand, the driver is going too fast in your opinion, a good option is using body language to express your terror at the life-threatening situation you feel you've been put in. Grabbing on to the seat or the dashboard, accompanied by a sharp, rapid intake of breath can be much more effective than anything you can say.

Lane Changing Advice. You're really in a better position to assess which lane the driver should be driving in. Start off with the assumption it's not the one he's driving in currently. As an impartial advisor you're not emotionally invested in any particular lane, unlike the driver.

Advanced Techniques

Be the "Extra Pair of Eyes" for the Driver. Four eyes are better than two. You never know when the driver will be distracted and not notice oncoming cross traffic. The following maneuver is best performed from the front seat. Lean forward to help the driver find the right moment to pull across the intersection or make that left turn. If done correctly, this technique simultaneously blocks the driver's view of the traffic, while insulting his judgment.

Your Duties as Copilot. In order to enable the driver to devote his entire attention to driving, it is your duty as back-seat driver/assistant to assume control of all secondary responsibilities. These include changing climate control, radio or CD selections and volume from what they were when originally selected by the driver to what they should be according to your judgment, which is not clouded by primary driving functions. You are also in charge of food and beverage consumption, singing, complaining and calling out, "5-0."

But your most important role as copilot is to control the maps, navigate, and give clear and concise directions to a driver depending on you to tell him where to go.

Helpful Phrases You'll Need When You're Navigating

"You were supposed to turn left back there."

"That was our exit."

"Where are you going?"

Did You Know?

The Buddha, having finally eliminated all ego from his consciousness and on his way to being taken up to Nirvana as a pure being of blissful oneness with the universe, was gently reminded of a car turning left in front of him by his most beloved disciple, who was riding in the back seat. Buddha turned on his disciple and screamed, "I SEE the goddman car!! Do you think I'm BLIND??!!" As a result, instead of achieving Nirvana, the Buddha was reincarnated as a frog, and had to start the cycle of birth/death/reincarnation all over again.[6]

---

[6] Eventually, after many lives, he was able to eliminate his ego again, and finally achieved Nirvana, but on the second, successful journey, he walked to his appointment rather than driving, so as to avoid a repeat of his earlier mistake.

Summary

Even when the driver knows the way, for example, to his own home, it's still your responsibility to give detailed directions on how to get there. On the other hand, if he doesn't know his way and you do, make him ask at every turn.

CHAPTER 25

Car Alarms: Say Hello to Your Neighbors

If you've moved into a new house or apartment in a new neighborhood and you want to meet your neighbors, or if you just want to remind your current neighbors you're still around, it may be time to buy a car alarm.

Choosing a Car Alarm That Will Be Most Disruptive

There are many features available to you when choosing an alarm. You should choose one which

Definitely:
→ goes off occasionally for no reason at all.
→ can only be deactivated by you pressing a button, especially when you're miles away.

Preferably:
→ features multiple noises such as honk and simultaneous siren.
→ automatically stops after about a minute, raising hopes in the neighborhood that the disturbance is over, then starts up again.
→ includes verbal harassment feature triggered by anyone in the near vicinity and also passing cars, loud music, other car alarms, pets, whistling and rain.
→ frequently can't be turned off at all, even by you.

(Note: If you have a lot of important things to do, you may want to choose an alarm which has a sound-while-driving option. This will encourage other drivers to get out of your way.)

There are other reasons to have a car alarm besides just pissing off your neighbors. A car alarm can also be very useful in public places. A good place to park is right outside an open mike night or poetry reading. Also possible: an intimate, romantic little restaurant where your ex-spouse may happen to be dining with a new love interest. Of course the main reason for purchasing a car alarm is still to park outside a golf or tennis match, your boss' kid's piano recital, or a party you weren't invited to.

Summary

Car alarms are expensive, but you'll sleep better at night knowing that your car is protected, especially if it's parked at least three and a half blocks away from where you're sleeping, so you won't be bothered when it goes off. You can turn it off in the morning.

PAGE 130

Thank you for visiting page 130, the "Documentation Verification Window," a subsection of "**Chapter 8, Making Your Visit to the DMV Successful.**" We are serving customers in the order of their ticket numbers. Your number is 2158. We are currently serving number 1345. Please have a seat. We will be with you shortly.

If you have waited all afternoon, you may approach the window now.

May we see your ticket please?

Your ticket is green. This is the orange ticket window. You need to go to the green ticket window which is located on page 181.

Please go now to page 181. Thank you.

CHAPTER 26

Tailgating: How Close Is Not Close Enough?

Calculating the Appropriate Distance You Should Leave Between You (You) and the Car Ahead of You (Them)

Start with one car length for every 10 m.p.h., add or subtract from there:

Distance to Add or Subtract	Reason for Adding or Subtracting
Minus five feet:	Them going too slowly
Minus five feet:	Them starting and stopping too much
Minus seven feet:	Them leaving their turn signal on too long
Minus eight feet:	You being in a hurry
Minus five feet:	You being in a bad mood
Plus two feet:	Bumper sticker for your favorite baseball team, band or candidate on their vehicle

Minus 10 feet:	Bumper sticker for your *least* favorite baseball team, band or candidate on their vehicle
Minus two feet:	You losing your job
Minus six feet:	Your significant other leaving you
Plus five feet:	Your significant other calls: it's back on
Minus five feet:	A kickass song is blasting on your stereo
Minus four feet:	You find the color of their car displeasing
Minus five feet:	It's hot outside
Minus three feet:	It's a weekday

Once you've determined the appropriate distance between you and the car you're following, you need to make another calculation to determine how aggressively you should be driving.

Formula for Your Aggression Index, or AI

1. Find a numerical value, on a scale of one to five, for Relative Importance of Your Time (RIT).

For example, you must decide, relative to the other drivers on the road, just how important you are and how valuable your time is. How important are the people you're meeting, the places you're going, the things you're doing?

2. Determine how late you are (L), and how bad the traffic is (T).

3. Assign a value to how much the other drivers on the road are pissing you off, or the pissoff ratio (POR).

4. Estimate an integer corresponding to how much you really have left to live for anyway (lfa).

By simply multiplying (RIT) (L) (T) and (POR), and dividing the product of (lfa) and Pi squared, you determine your Aggression Index for any particular situation:

$$AI = \frac{(RIT)\ (L)\ (T)\ (POR)}{(lfa)\ \pi^2}$$

Once you've found a value for your Aggression Index, multiply it by how much stress was generated by the process of its calculation, and take it all out on the driver in front of you.

Dealing with Tailgaters

Since you normally travel a conservative 15 to 20 miles an hour above the speed limit, you won't have too much trouble with tailgaters yourself, but it can happen. Having a tailgater behind you is a frightening and dangerous situation which must be handled with maturity and poise.

Incorrect	**Correct**
Allow them to scare you into accelerating up to an unsafe speed.	Safely change lanes to let the tailgater pass, then immediately return to your original lane and tailgate that f**ker for the next 15 miles.

The Unsung Heroism of the American Tailgater

Should a crash take place when you are tailgating, really it's you who's going to go crashing through the windshield. The guy in front will probably be all right, in spite of his phony claims of "whiplash" injuries. By tailgating, you show you're willing to sacrifice your own body for what you believe in, for what is right, for what is good.

Adding insult to injury, the laws devised by the croissant-swallowing socialists at the DMV are stacked in favor of the sociopath who is driving too slowly in the fast lane. When foolish drivers try to clog our nation's vital arteries by driving too slowly, it's the tailgaters who step into the front lines. When mindless Sunday drivers leave their blinkers on for miles at a time, it's the tailgaters who let their voices be heard. It is that same spirit which created heroes like Rosa Parks, Martin Luther King Jr., and Justin Timberlake. And yet the term "tailgater" is used as a pejorative label, devaluing a patriotic social movement. It is this name-calling and these scare tactics which have always been used to demonize dissenters. If we let this happen, the terrorists win.

Summary

Good drivers should note that there are places where tailgating does not exist. In France, they have no word for "tailgater." The closest match would be the phrase, "coller au pare-chocs," which can be loosely translated as "bathes infrequently."

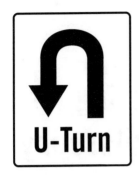

U-Turn

Emergency Situations Guide

Keep this vital step-by-step guide in your car, *where you can reach it* at all times, in case of an emergency. We hope you'll never need it, but it's good to know it's there.

What to Do If:

Your brakes go out going down a steep hill . . .

Gee, that's a tough one. Hmmm. What if . . . no, that wouldn't work. Let us think about this, and we'll get back to you.

Your accelerator gets stuck on the freeway going 85 . . .

Gosh, these are hard. Does that really happen to people?

You go into an uncontrolled skid on icy road . . .

What are you doing driving around on an icy road? Didn't it occur to you that driving on ice might be a *bad* idea?

Your cell phone goes out in the middle of an important call . . .

Hook the charger up to your cigarette lighter and recharge. You did bring your charger, right? . . . RIGHT!?!

Now, are you still heading down that steep hill with no brakes? . . .

Still drawing a blank on this one. Let's think here. Brakes go out on hill, brakes go out on a hill . . . Nope. We can't think of anything. You're on your own. Good luck.

CHAPTER 27

The Zen of Driving, or Driving and Philosophy

One of the most ancient and profound questions of philosophy is the famous Zen koan:

→ If you roll through a stop sign and there are NO COPS there to see it, have you broken the law?

It is not the only unanswerable question. Another profound puzzle where physics and philosophy meet is:

→ If one must always cross the halfway point when traveling between point A and point B, and when it has been crossed, one must again cross a new halfway point between the midpoint (now C) and point B in an infinite journey which by definition can never be completed, why am I always getting into accidents?

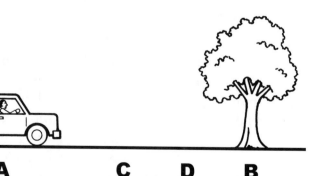

A   **C**   **D**   **B**

Another imponderable:

→ What the hell's with those "Runaway Truck Ramps?" Come on, if your brakes go out on a big hill when you're in a semi, you're screwed, and so is everyone ahead of you. Does that *happen* a lot? Is this *common??*

Contemplating any of these questions in a calm, meditative state can lead to a life-changing insight, heralded by a choir of angels and the sound of heavenly trumpets. Or it could be the light has turned green, and a lot of people are honking at you.

Another enlightening paradox to ponder is:

How come it's OK for you to drive like a total a**hole, and yet it is so horribly annoying when other people do exactly the same thing?

In the same way the Zen master contemplates eternal paradoxes like, "What is the sound of one hand clapping?" possibly for an entire lifetime before unlocking the truths hidden in the puzzle or determining it's a really stupid question, the Zen driver finds eternal paradoxes in ordinary-appearing yet infinitely ambiguous road signs, like:

"SLOW," "CAUTION," "DO NOT PASS," and "WRONG WAY"

The Zen driver knows that what is "wrong" to fringe, left-wing Communists like Jacques Chirac and Kofi Annan is apple pie to gun-toting redneck hicks like Tom Delay, and a delicately nuanced interplay of right and wrong to fair-minded independents like Bill O'Reilly.

Upon realizing that these signs mean nothing and everything simultaneously, the Zen driver concludes the safest thing to do is ignore them completely.

Summary

If God knows all, He already knows that you're about to run that red light, and thus you have no free will in the matter. This is always a winning argument to raise in traffic court.

If you have free will, then God doesn't know you're going to run the light; He might be speeding through the intersection Himself talking on His cell phone, and you could hit Him. You'd better have a pretty good lawyer if you're going to get into an accident with God.

CHAPTER 28

Motorcycles: Faster, Cooler, Safer!

There's a lot of needless hysteria going around on the subject of riding motorcycles, most of it generated by so called "research" that identifies riding a motorcycle as the number one best way to become a vegetable. But these so-called researchers make their wild charges based on statistics which overlook many important facts. Like how much fun it is, how cool you look, and the fact that none of the researchers are themselves vegetables. How do they know it's such a bad thing if they've never even tried it?

Bad News

Technically, you're not supposed to ride between and weave in and out of cars to speed through a traffic jam.

Good News

You'll never know that, because you stopped reading at the word "technically," cause it's not your kind of word, and it didn't sound like the kind of sentence you'd be interested in reading.

More Good News

You get to wear black leather motorcycle jackets and pants with lots and lots of zippers. Also boots.

More Bad News

Some states require that you wear a motorcycle helmet, which throws off the whole cool theme you had going with the leather.

Starting Your Own Motorcycle Gang

Of course it can get kind of lonely on the road, just you and your bike, so sooner or later you will want to start your own outlaw motorcycle gang. But first you'll need to find an intimidating name for your gang.

Good Names	Bad Names
Satan's Butt-Kicking Hooligans	Two Wheel Adventure Club
Hell's Heathens	Bob & Eileen's Sunset Riders
Death's Commandos	Bikers for Social Justice
Lucifer's Outlaws	Leisure World Cycling Society
Psycho Sadist Serial Killers	Bike, Hike & Swim Experience
Axis of Evil	The Bing Crosby Motorcycle Fellowship

Summary

It is unknown why, but there are several advantages to motorcyle riding which many bikers are unaware of. For example, technically, you are allowed to ride in the car pool lane.

U-Turn

Offensive Driving

There's plenty of information available for the weak-minded about so-called "defensive driving." In fact the dope-sniffing sex fiends at the DMV would like everyone to be a defensive driver. But if nobody's on offense, there is no game.

To break down a defense you must be faster, quicker and smarter. You must be constantly on the attack, calling audibles, running trick plays, anticipating their strategies, knowing their weaknesses. Offensive drivers should always:

→ Assume all other drivers can see you perfectly at all times and in all driving conditions.

→ Assume they know what you're about to do. Try to surprise them.

But the best offensive driving is *proactive*. Instead of merely reacting, the offensive driver engages in *preemptive bad driving*, anticipating problematic situations before they occur.

Preemptive Bad Driving

The preemptive bad driver takes action to prevent potential tragedies such as having to drive too slowly *before* they materialize. By *preemptive tailgating*, you send a message that slow driving will not be tolerated. You could wait for the driver to drive slowly, but by then it may be too late. The smoking gun may come in the form of you having to drive 45 m.p.h. in the fast lane.

Another essential is *preemptive honking*. Say you're stopped at a light behind someone who represents a gathering threat to not notice when the light changes. By preemptive honking before the light changes, you make sure that driver will be ready when it does.

There is also *preemptive verbal harassment*. By leaning out your window and yelling profanities at the drivers in the next lane, you reduce the likelihood that they will do something that would have deserved those profanities later.

CHAPTER 29

Dismantling the DMV Agenda: A Global Perspective

Censeurée

This chapter has been censored by the DMV.
To protect national security, sensitive
information has been redacted.

are advised to remain calm

were released to us as
a result of the Freedom of Information Act

but ███████████████████████████████████
██
██
████et ████████. ███████████████████████
██
██████ but ██████████████████████████████
██
████████████████████████████ huge quantities
of which were dumped into our drinking water. ████████
██
████████████████████. ███████████████████
██
██████████████████ m. ████████████████████
████████████████ in a revealing negligee
██
██
██
██████. ████ not even legal in Texas ████████████
██
██
██
██
████████████ consenting adults ████████████
██
██
██
██████s████████████████████████████████
██
██
████████████████████████████████ not "just
a frog" to me ███████████████████████████
██
██

▬▬▬ ▬▬▬ ▬▬▬▬▬ ▬▬▬▬▬▬▬ overwhelming
evidence that George W. Bush ▬▬▬ ▬▬▬▬▬▬▬▬
▬▬▬▬ ▬▬▬▬ ▬ ▬▬▬▬▬▬ ▬▬▬▬▬▬
▬▬▬▬▬ ▬▬▬▬ ▬▬▬▬▬ ▬▬▬▬ ▬▬▬.
▬▬▬▬▬ ▬▬▬▬ ▬▬▬▬▬ ▬▬▬▬ ▬▬▬▬▬
▬▬▬▬▬ ▬▬▬▬▬ ▬ ▬▬▬▬▬▬ ▬ ▬▬ ▬▬▬▬
▬▬▬▬ ▬▬▬▬▬ ▬▬▬▬▬▬ now awaiting the
go-ahead to invade Earth ▬▬▬▬▬ ▬▬▬▬▬ ▬▬▬
▬▬▬ ▬ ▬▬▬▬▬ ▬▬▬▬▬ ▬▬▬▬▬ ▬▬▬▬
▬▬▬ ▬▬ ▬▬▬▬ ▬▬▬. ▬▬▬▬ ▬▬▬▬▬▬
▬▬▬▬▬ ▬▬▬ ▬▬▬▬▬ ▬▬▬▬▬. W▬▬▬ ▬▬▬
▬▬▬▬▬ ▬ ▬▬▬▬ ▬ ▬▬▬▬▬ ▬▬▬ ▬▬▬▬▬▬
▬▬▬ ▬▬▬▬ ▬▬▬ ▬ ▬▬▬▬▬ ▬▬▬▬▬ ▬▬▬. ▬▬▬ ▬▬
▬▬▬ ▬▬▬▬ ▬▬▬▬▬ ▬▬▬ what appears to be a relative
of the Armadillo family. ▬▬▬▬ ▬▬▬▬▬ ▬ ▬▬
▬▬ ▬▬▬▬▬ ▬▬. ▬▬▬▬ ▬▬▬ ▬▬ ▬▬▬▬
▬▬▬▬▬ ▬▬▬▬▬▬ ▬▬▬ ▬▬▬▬ ▬▬▬
submerged in the kitty litter ▬▬▬▬ ▬▬ ▬▬▬▬▬ ▬▬
▬▬▬▬▬ ▬▬▬▬ ▬▬▬ ▬▬▬▬ ▬▬▬▬▬ ▬
▬▬. ▬▬▬ ▬▬▬▬▬ ▬▬▬ ▬▬▬▬ ▬▬▬▬▬
▬▬ ▬▬▬ ▬▬▬▬ ▬▬ ▬▬▬▬ ▬▬▬▬ ▬▬▬▬
▬ ▬▬▬ ▬ ▬▬▬ ▬ ▬▬▬▬ ▬▬▬▬ ▬ ▬▬▬
▬▬▬▬ ▬▬ ▬▬▬ ▬▬▬▬▬ ▬▬▬▬ because the
DMV for many years has been plotting to ▬▬▬ ▬▬▬ ▬▬
▬▬▬▬ ▬▬▬ ▬▬▬ ▬▬▬▬ ▬▬▬ ▬▬▬▬ o▬▬▬▬
▬▬▬. ▬▬▬▬ ▬ ▬▬ ▬▬▬▬ ▬▬▬ ▬ ▬▬▬▬
▬▬. ▬▬▬ ▬▬ ▬▬ 40 second keg stand ▬▬▬▬
▬▬▬ ▬ ▬▬▬▬ 11 ▬▬ ▬▬▬ ▬▬▬▬ ▬▬▬▬ ▬
▬▬▬ ▬▬▬▬. W▬▬ ▬▬▬ ▬▬▬▬ ▬▬ ▬▬▬ ▬
▬▬▬▬▬ ▬▬▬ ▬▬ ▬▬▬ ▬▬▬ ▬▬▬ ▬
▬▬ ▬▬▬ ▬▬▬▬ ▬▬ ▬ ▬▬▬ ▬▬▬▬
▬▬ ▬▬▬▬ ▬▬ ▬▬▬ ▬▬▬ ▬▬▬ ▬▬ ▬▬▬
▬ ▬▬▬▬▬. ▬▬▬ ▬▬▬ ▬▬▬ ▬▬▬ ▬▬▬

████ ██ ████ ██ never heard from again. ████████████
██
██
██ ████████
████████ ████████s████████ now controlling the body
of Jimmy Carter.

CHAPTER 30

You Are What You Drive

You often hear that people resemble their pets. It's not so different with cars. The cars people drive often match the characteristics of their owners. Can you match these cars with a brief description of their owners?

Description

Tailgater

Not good at left turns

Now where did I put my coffee?

Frequent sudden stopper

Besides the condition of your car there are other ways to announce who you are.

What the Music You Play Says About You

Music	Played Quietly	Played Very Loudly
Classical	Big loser	Cross dresser
Heavy Metal	Disturbed individual	What?
Rap	Busted speakers	Rear left speaker fixed, still working on the others
Opera	Serious mental problems	Serious mental problems

Summary

You can make adjustments to your image without buying a new car. For example, California Governor Arnold Schwarzenegger has had one of his Hummer's retooled as a hybrid, which boosts his mileage to an eco-friendly 11 mpg, saving 600 gallons of gas per year. However, to avoid appearing too much like what political scientists call a "girlie-man," he pours the saved gasoline and also his dirty oil directly into the Sacramento River.

PAGE 149

Thank you for visiting page 149, the "Transfer of Ownership Station" a subsection of **"Chapter 8, Making Your Visit to the DMV Successful."**

Please get in the back of the long line of other drivers waiting to see an agent at the "Transfer of Ownership Station." Your wait should be approximately 15 minutes longer than the time we estimate, which is approximately 25 minutes.

Have you waited 40 minutes yet? Wait another 10 minutes.

OK, it's your turn now. What is your number?

You don't have a number? You should have a number. Didn't you check in at the "General Information Window?" We're sorry, but all visitors to the DMV must first go to the "General Information Window," which is located on page 96.

Please go now to page 96. Thank you.

CHAPTER 31

Sex and Driving: Completely Unrelated Concepts? Not If You're the Donkey

Before having sex with someone, you can gather clues about your compatibility by observing certain things about them.

Things Women Should Note	Things Men Should Note
Will he wear a seat belt?	Can she handle a stick shift?
Does he floor the accelerator?	Does she overuse the brake?
Can he shift gears?	Can you go to sleep after a long drive, or do you have to talk?
Will he ask for directions?	Is she willing to have sex with you?

If the signs are satisfactory, you can go ahead and have sex. However, if you're looking for something more serious like a long-term relationship, you'll need to pay particular attention to the more serious, long term section of this chapter, designed for the mature adult:

Choosing a Mate: Do You Have Any Idea How Much More Time You'll Spend Driving Together Than Having Sex? (Do the Math—Driving's More Important)

OK. Have you done the math yet? Now take the time you've estimated you'll be driving together and double it. Take the time you estimate you'll be having sex and cut it in half. This is beginning to get a bit more realistic. You can see why driving compatibility is so important.

It is possible, with effort, counseling and faith to overcome such relatively minor bumps on the road to a happy marriage or long-term relationship as infidelity or domestic violence, but if both partners insist on being the one to drive, the relationship is doomed. A lack of sexual chemistry can be overcome, but if one partner is a fast, aggressive tailgater and the other partner is a meandering, absent-minded dawdler behind the wheel, it's just not going to happen. Most dating services ask unimportant questions like, "What is your idea of a perfect date?" All well and good, but if "long, romantic walks along the beach" is your reply, unless you happen to be a fish, you're going to have to drive to the beach first. And that's why we're offering the first and only:

Bad Driver's Dating Service

Simply fill out the following questionnaire, and e-mail responses to us at www.thebaddrivershandbook.com, and we'll pass it on to other single bad drivers of the gender you're looking for in your area.

Age:_____

Gender:_____

Sexual orientation:_____

Location (area):_____

You would describe your feelings about pedestrians as:
A) controlled animosity.
B) passionate dislike.
C) furious loathing.

If I'm lost, I will consult a map:
A) in desperate circumstances.
B) under no circumstances.
C) when pigs fly over the *Champs Élysées*.

The average difference between your speed and the "speed limit" is:
A) 10%
B) 20%
C) more than 40% but will consider dating someone in category A) or B)

My idea of a perfect date includes:
A) minor damage to public property.
B) candle-lit road-kill dinner.
C) long, romantic police car chase on a lonely beach at sunset.
D) roasting marshmallows over a vehicle fire.

Personality type I'm looking for:
A) Aggressive
B) Impatient
C) Intolerant

Write about you and your driving habits here. Be sure to include some of the worst things you've done as a driver. (No more than 6 pages.)

Optional: photograph of yourself.
Required: photograph of your car. (attach to e-mail)

Truly, Actually Really Bad Drivers (Not in the Bad-but-Actually-Good Sense, but in the Definitely, Frighteningly Bad Sense)

CHAPTER 32

How to Tell Your Friend or Relative He's a Really, Truly Bad Driver (Besides Getting Him This Book)

The Greeting Card

We all know there's no better way to express your own unique, deeply personal feelings about someone you care for than with a mass-produced brand name greeting card. Here's one for a romantic interest:

Roses Are Red, Violets Are Blue,

*You're a Really Shi**y Driver*

And I'm Afraid You're Going to Kill Yourself,

So Please Get a Bicycle.

Try this one on Grandma:

You baked me cookies and gave me your love,

You read me stories and made me feel so special,

The Angels in Heaven sent you to me, Grandma.

But your eyesight is failing you and I think you're

an extremely dangerous driver so I sold your car.

Conversation Starters

A good way to start this delicate subject is with a compliment or positive observation:

"Have you lost weight? You *have* lost weight! Speaking of losing weight, your driving is truly, truly terrible. Just awful."

"You're really athletic. I bet you'd be good at skateboarding. Which you should really try, because you're a frighteningly bad driver."

"You'll never know how much I love you. I'd even ride in a car you were driving. I love you that much."

"Hey, look what I found! Just lying on the ground! A bus pass with your name on it. Take it. Please!"

"It's so silly of us to be afraid to fly when statistics show the chances of getting in an accident are so much greater driving to and from the airport. Especially if *you're* driving."

"Isn't it amazing how everybody has different abilities. For example, some people are good drivers. In your case, it's fooseball."

Other Methods

Still not getting through? Try:

Summary

If all else fails, put a boot on their car and let them figure it out.

CHAPTER 33

The Mature Driver: Driving When You Can No Longer See

As a member of today's more vigorous senior citizenry, you are healthier, more fit, more active and more competent to drive later into your life span than any previous generation. Moreover, most cars have only two pedals so you have a 50% chance of hitting the right one.

Why Driving Slow Is a Good Thing

Like other road signs, speed limits either have second meanings or don't apply to senior citizens.

If you are 65 or older, you qualify for the Senior Discount. Go ahead and take 15% off the speed limit to calculate what speed you're supposed to be going. Thus, if the speed limit is 65, and 15% of 65 is roughly 20, and 65 minus 20 is approximately 40, you should travel at 40 miles per hour.

What you're really doing is compensating for all the speeding the rest of us are doing. We as people, *on average* do not drive over the speed limit when you factor in senior citizens doing their part.

Driving slowly not only adds to diversity on our highways, but reminds us of a simpler time in our history when music videos didn't have 200 jump cuts per minute, movies cost 25 cents, and smoking was healthy.

Finally, driving slowly is good because . . . what was the question?

Your Family Hates You

Don't let them take your keys.

It's the first step. Your family's been plotting your demise for some time now. The keys are always the first to go. First the keys, then the car, then the furniture, pretty soon you'll be eating baby food out of a dinosaur-patterned baby dish in a nursing home where everyone pretends you're crazy. Even when you say simple stuff like, "Thursday is when the cat tells me what to wear," they'll look at you as if they don't understand what you mean, all with the intention of making you think you are crazy so they can take your stuff. Ask them, "Why are the nurses trying to kill me?" and say good-bye to your car. Explain to them that the Jerries have taken over the kitchen, they'll just smile and your house will be on the market by morning. This is why it's important when they talk to you and you can't hear them to just nod and say "yes." When a blurry, ambiguous relative walks in, just refer to it as "dear." No names are necessary.

You might not need any help becoming a bad driver. If you can pass the Senility Test, then you can go ahead driving, assuming your technique is well developed.

Senility Test

You can remember you own name:
A) Always
B) Sometimes
C) Never

If you answered B) or C), you're good to go.

Can you recognize immediate family members?
A) Yes
B) No
C) More soup

If you answered B) or C), get behind the wheel and take the road, it's yours.

The people were here, someone stole my sweater.
A) That's not a question.
B) Yes
C) Well, I don't know.

If you answered B) or C), drive to the pharmacy, pick up your meds.

You're Not Getting Older, You're Getting Smaller

The fact that you're getting shorter as well as progressively blinder and more confused is actually a formidable weapon when used properly. Hunker down so that your gray head is barely above the dashboard, which you can emphasize by grabbing the steering wheel near the top.

Now roll up to that four-way stop sign and keep on rolling! Other drivers will stop for you! They will think you can't see.

You are that much closer to achieving that holiest of bad driver fantasies: never having to use the brake pedal.

Driving Tips When You *Really* Can No Longer See

1. Avoid all blurry objects of any kind.
2. Use your other senses. (Your hearing is probably not too good so rely on your *sense of smell.*) (Note: if you smell burning, you may have hit something, if you don't, you're probably OK.)
3. Your seeing-eye dog can be a big help.

4. Be confident. Think about all the great achievements of other blind people. Think Helen Keller, think Stevie Wonder, think Ray Charles. Think Jordi from *Star Trek: the Next Generation.*

Safety Tip

If you are relying primarily on your sense of smell, don't get behind the wheel when you have a bad cold.

Summary

If you're a mature driver and you've just completed reading this chapter, we're sure you'll agree it contains so much useful information it's really a shame you've already forgotten it. Maybe you should read it again.

CHAPTER 34

Sleeping at the Wheel: Do's and Don'ts

The ultimate test of multi-tasking skills is driving while asleep. *Caution:* don't attempt this advanced skill until you've mastered beginning and intermediate multi-tasking skills like driving and shaving, eating, reading, writing, knitting, applying make-up and conducting chemistry experiments. If you have a job which demands long hours like working in the movie industry on all-day shoots, being an air traffic controller or working in the field of emergency medicine, you will need to develop the ability to sleep while driving home. Here are some tips:

Don't
Drink caffeinated beverages such as coffee and CocaCola which can make you jittery and disrupt your transition into sleep mode.

Do
Have a commuter cup of warm milk and honey to help you drift off into dreamland.

Do
Take advantage of shorter, more numerous naps. Several short naps of just a couple of minutes can be as refreshing as a long sleep.

Don't

Dream about driving while you're asleep at the wheel. That defeats the whole purpose, and you'll wake up even more tired and stressed than when you nodded off.

Do

Turn off cell phones, two-way pagers and other devices which could disturb your slumber.

Don't

Rest your head on the horn.

Do

Pick at least two lanes to weave back and forth between. Studies show sleeping drivers need two to three times more space than drivers who are fully awake.

Don't

Veer off the road. Hitting stationary objects can be more disruptive to your sleep than caffeine.

Do

Leave twice as much space between you and the car in front of you than you would leave if you were awake. Studies show sleeping drivers need at least twice as much time to react to braking vehicles.

Summary

While human evolution has not produced a survival instinct to wake us up if we fall asleep at the wheel, fortunately it *has* produced a survival instinct to wake us up if we sense the presence of a hungry mastodon. Isn't evolution a funny thing? Not funny like ha-ha funny, but funny like strange but true, quirky/useless, smashed-into-a-tree, broken-skull funny.

Ten Essential Items for Your Car

Essential Item	Purpose
Mannequin	Car pool lane
Support Your Local Police sticker	Unplanned interaction with law enforcement
Thing that you've been looking for the last two years	Lifting your spirits
13-week-old parking ticket	Maybe they'll forget
9-week-old French fries	When passengers get hungry
Copy of *"Bad Driver's Handbook"*	Self improvement
Emergency flares	Something for the kiddies to play with
Night vision goggles	You could be called on a secret mission
3 Bon Jovi Albums	Oh, someone must have left those here. They're not mine, I swear.
Life-sized Bon Jovi Poster	No seriously, that stuff is not mine!

CHAPTER 35

Really Bad Driver's Rehab

At it's most virulent, bad driving is a powerful disease. It's helpful to know that even successful people whom we all respect
can fall victim to it. Here is an actual, verbatim confession from
a real recovering bad driver. This is a person who is actually a
well-known politician, often noted for his bad driving. To protect his anonymity, we've changed his name from Senator John
McCain of Arizona to John McCarthy (not his real name.)[7]

"JOHN McCARTHY"
Hi. My name is "John McCarthy." I am a bad
Driver.

SUPPORT GROUP
Hi, John!

"JOHN McCARTHY"
I'm 115 days good driving. But I still feel if I
were to run just one stop sign, it would all come
back to me. It's a slippery slope. Some people
can tailgate one or two cars and forget about it.
But for others, like me, it's never enough. Faster,
faster, faster! More, more, more! Once I
thought I was just a social bad driver, but now

---

[7] "McCain Puts the Pedal to the Medal" *Washington Post* 05/15/04

I know, probably because of genetic factors, this disease will always be with me.

Senator "John McCarthy" found power and strength through these confidential confessions, and also through a recovery process we call:

Twelve-Step Program for Really Bad Drivers

1. Admit you are powerless over bad driving and your life has become unmanageable.
2. Acknowledge existence of a Higher Power.
3. Allow other driver to cut you off. (Rely on Higher Power to exact revenge on this s.o.b.)
4. Suppress urge to yell "A**hole!!" at driver going too slow in fast lane. Instead, breathe deeply, smile and wave, resting easy because Higher Power will punish slow driver in Hell.
5. Practice coming to full and complete stop at STOP signs.
6. That was not a full and complete stop. Remember, Higher Power is watching you!
7. It was pretty Goddamn close to a full stop! What the Hell do you people want from me?!
8. Don't use Higher Power's name in vain. Higher Power is getting upset with you.
9. Review progress so far, decide if you are ready for new life in recovery.
10. Decide you are not yet ready.
11. Renounce Higher Power, acknowledge existence of Lower Power.
12. Cut off other driver in lane next to you.

Summary for Really Bad Drivers

In the recovery process, it's helpful to find other, healthy outlets for your aggression. Could you join a street gang? Is there someone in your family you could take out your aggression on, like a parent, child or spouse? Perhaps an armed visit to a place of former employment would help. How about breaking things?

CHAPTER 36

Pull Over to the Right and Stop Your Vehicle: Ambulances, Fire Trucks, and Student Drivers

What a nuisance some of our silly laws are. It's like they make these things up just to make your life harder. Technically, you are "supposed to" pull over to the side of the road every time you hear a siren. Remember:

→ If you don't hear the siren, it's perfectly legal to keep on driving.

With this in mind, a good way to reduce the number of times you have to do this is to play your car stereo so loud that you can't hear these sirens. People with important things to do like you can't afford all the wasted time. And with all those other people pulled over to the side of the road, this is an excellent time to move ahead.

On the other hand, if you're the type of person who likes a little excitement, you can be assured that the action is where the fire trucks, the ambulance and the cops are going. Follow that siren and you're sure to catch a daring rescue, a burning building, a bank robbery/shoot-out, or at least a good old harassment of a minority or homeless person.

You should do this because A) it provides a little real-world excitement lacking in most people's lives, but more importantly B) they may need your help. Drive around with First Aid kits, buckets of water, a ladder or two and whatever kind of weapons you can pull together. Cops really appreciate your help! So when you see a car chase, pull in behind one cop car and in front an another, and off you go! Or help clear the road for a fire truck by getting out in front and honking your horn.

Paramedics in particular appreciate medical advice from knowledgeable civilians like yourself. Be confident and concise when you give directions to them in emergencies. Try:

"I wouldn't do that."

"That doesn't look like it's working."

"Where are you going with this?"

The only emergency situation in which you should always pull over to the right and stop your vehicle is when you see a student driver. Student drivers can be identified by their tendency to ignore lane markings, road signs, other cars, and sidewalks, as well as the look of panic on the face of the driving instructor or family member riding in the front passenger seat. When you see the look, pull over immediately and wait five minutes before getting back on the road.

Summary

The ranking order of emergency priorities is: all civilian drivers pull over for cops, cops pull over for ambulances, ambulances pull over for fire trucks, but they all cower in the presence of the student driver.

CHAPTER 37

Taxi Drivers: How Do You Say, "Watch Out!" in Farsi?

Here are a few helpful phrases you'll need when traveling by taxi:

English	Farsi
Watch out!	آق ٿۇظغغق ن!
Slow down!	ۇۋ رضقۀي!
Red light!	ض آؤٿقۀ!
Car!	ۂغئ!
Wall!	ثؤئ!
This is not the way to the airport!	هتخ!
Ahhhhhhhhh!	Aiiiyyyiiiieeeeeeeee!

Summary

Taking a taxi is like taking a magical vacation in the Middle East, only more dangerous.

CHAPTER 38

Illustrated History of Bad Driving

While rummaging through ancient texts and documents, we found surprising evidence that the roots of bad driving in its earliest forms extend back in time way before our current era.

A page taken from the recently discovered *Bad Horseman's Handbook* shows proper execution of what today we call "The Jerk Merge Left" (see page 16), but was then called "The Scoundrel's Hot Foot Turn."

The Scoundrel's Hot Foot Turn

The following wall relief was found on the tomb of Tutankhamen in the Valley of the Kings. The hieroglyphics explain that Tutankahamen (left) was not at fault because the

High Priest in front of him made an unexpected full stop at a stop sign.

The High Priest was brutally executed for risking Tutankhamen's safety with such a dangerous maneuver.

This next item is from the rarely referenced illustration section of the Old Testament:

Joshua, who was an extremely impatient driver, is seen in the center of this illustration (arrow) improperly using his horn to express his frustration with the flow of traffic. This caused a lot of honking and shouting amongst the other drivers unto each other, and the walls of the city of Jericho crumbled as a result. This was a very good thing, as clearly indicated by the text below the illustration, which reads: "And they utterly destroyed all that was in the city, both man and woman, young and old, and ox, and sheep, and ass, with the edge of the sword" (Joshua 6:21). Even back in Biblical times, bad drivers were known to be testy.

Summary

These documents, previously suppressed by agents of the International DMV Conspiracy, show that they can burn the evidence, but the truth will come out, and make an illegal left turn.

CHAPTER 39

Bad Driving in the Future

The following chronology of future events in bad driving was compiled by some avid readers of *The Farmer's Almanac.*

2010: DMV lobbyists in the U.S. Congress propose smart highway system with computer technology embedded in highways to connect with onboard computers in cars. Proposal stalls in Senate Transportation Committee.

2014: DMV dissolves U.S. Congress, English Parliament, all other legislative bodies; sets up World Government headquartered in Paris, France.

2015: Smart highway system introduced. Smart asphalt now more intelligent than 68% of U.S. population.[8]

2016: DMV World Government requires mandatory autopilot for all vehicles to be used on smart highways.

2018: Bad drivers revolt, sabotage smart highway/autopilot system.

---

[8] 17% jump from survey taken Nov. 2, 2004 when dumb asphalt was more intelligent than 51% of the U.S. population.

2024: DMV executes co-stars Vin Diesel and Paul Walker of *The Fast and the Furious* as display of power, warning to bad drivers.

2025: Vin Diesel becomes martyr; revolt spreads.

2030: New calendar introduced; year one is birth of Vin Diesel (old calendar year 1967).

65 AVD (*anno Vin Diesel*): DMV World Government overthrown by popular uprising. All motor vehicle laws canceled.

68 AVD: Vin Diesel's message of unconditional love and driving freedom spreads throughout universe.

71 AVD: Bicyclists banned from roadways, hover bicyclists still annoying.

Summary

Those who cannot remember the future are condemned to repeat it.

U-Turn

You Can Be a Bad Driver *Even While You're Sleeping!*

"But how," we hear you saying, "can I drive badly while I'm asleep?"

Incredibly, there is a perfectly good answer to this question, and it doesn't involve dreaming!

The secret is *bad parking*. And you can accomplish this *without* opening yourself up to a parking ticket! It's just a matter of proper equipment and careful car placement.

Simply take your oversized SUV, monster pickup truck or Hummer, making sure you have *darkly tinted windows*, and find a parking space on a busy boulevard next to an intersection with a stop sign. By careful positioning, you can place your vehicle in such a way that it is virtually impossible for a driver stopping at the stop sign to see past your parked car to check if it's safe to pull out. *And this is all perfectly legal!*

While it may be hard to believe, by making your parked car into a major visual obstruction for other drivers, you can cause a major accident *while you're asleep, in the comfort of your own home!*

Extra credit for artistic merit is given to those who, instead of taking their beat up old wreck down to the junkyard, brighten up the neighborhood by parking it on their lawn for a minimum of not less than one year.

CHAPTER 40

Drinking and Driving: Like Sex and Cheeseburgers— Both Good, but Not at the Same Time

There's nothing wrong with drinking. If God had not intended for us to drink, He would not have made sobriety so damn boring, painful and meaningless. Also, there's nothing unhealthy about drinking. Doctors say that a glass of red wine each night can be quite beneficial to your health. For those of us who prefer to take care of things all at once, fourteen glasses of red wine once every couple of weeks should have about the same salutary effect.

In fact there are few things in life that are more enjoyable than going on an all-night bender and waking up in a pool of your own piss and vomit on a barroom floor, street corner or jail cell. *However,* it is only the most amateur bad drivers who need to be drunk in order to drive badly. The true bad driver does not need alcohol or other performance-enhancing drugs. A drunk driver is not a bad driver, just a driver who is drunk. Drunk drivers give bad drivers a bad name. What they do is not bad driving, it's sloppy driving, unskilled, inattentive driving, unaware driving. The true bad driver is keenly aware of every-thing he is doing.

For those readers who may already have had too much to drink, the following chart will make what we are trying to say clear:

Activity	Assessment
Drinking	Good
Driving	Good
Sex	Good
Cheeseburgers	Good
Drinking & Driving	Bad
Drinking & Sex	Good
Drinking & Cheeseburgers	Very Good
Driving & Cheeseburgers	Good
Driving & Sex	Good
Sex and Cheeseburgers	Bad

Summary for Vegetarians

You may substitute "going hiking in the woods with a loved one" for "sex" in the above chart and the results should be the same.

PAGE 181

Merci beaucoup de la page visitante 181. Peux j'avoir votre nombre d'agent et sécréter le mot de passer?

Oh! You must be at ze wrong placement. Zis placement iz for ze French government officials and also ze United Nations. You 'av made a grande mistake. May I suggest you visit **"Chapter 8: Making Your Visit to the DMV Successful,"** located on ze page 51.

Merci beaucoup de la page visitante 181 . . . imbecile Americaine.

Va maintenant s'il vous plaît a la page 51. Merci.

CHAPTER 41

A Bunch of Stuff We Couldn't Really Find a Place for

As you read the following material, imagine that it is in some sort of context that makes it seem not only relevant, but also an interesting twist on the subject we'd just been talking about.

How to Conduct a Successful Police Car Chase Getaway

Go really fast. Maybe your beat up, stolen car will outpace the patrol cars, or they will run out of gas. Those helicopters must use up a lot of gas. They can't keep it up forever, they're bound to run out sooner or later.

In the unlikely event that you run out of gas before they do, try to take them on foot. You'll have a good shot at this too, because cops are fat and slow due to poor eating habits. You're probably faster than they are, and while they do have dogs, and dogs tend to be fairly quick, they are just dogs, and you're a human. Rely on your wits to deal with the dogs.

Bonus Tip: Cashing In

Call the manufacturer of your car during the chase, and ask how much they will pay you to keep it up. No publicity is bad publicity. You're guaranteed to be on the news during the entire duration of the chase—hours of free TV exposure for their brand, because the media has nothing more important to report on than your adventure. Remember O.J. Simpson and the White Bronco? That increased the sales not only of White Broncos but also of orange juice for years thereafter.

Did You Know?

→ If your car enters a railroad crossing before an oncoming train, you have the right of way. It is the train which must stop.

Myths & Urban Legends

Myth: Asian women are all bad drivers.

Truth: Not all Asian women are bad drivers. In fact many are good drivers, and some are better drivers than men. While Asian women are more genetically prone to be bad drivers (Summers, *Harvard Quarterly,* 2005), only an arrogant person would claim to know how any one individual will perform on the road.

Myth: Despite how dorky it looks for a teenager to drive with a seat belt, driving without one is unsafe.

Truth: It's not unsafe to drive without a seat belt as long as you're, like, totally not going to get into an accident.

Myth: Peer pressure can cause people to drive recklessly and at unsafe speeds.

Truth: Oh, come on, don't be such a wuss. Live a little.

Myth: Cops pull people over based on race alone.

Truth: Law enforcement officers do not give in to racial stereotypes, and will not stop a driver without probable cause, such as the uneasy feeling that the officer gets when he sees a black man in a nice car.

Myth: It's "bad luck" to pass on a two lane highway going uphill on a curve.
Truth: There is no scientific evidence to support the existence of "good" or "bad" luck.

Myth: Driving a stick shift is more masculine than driving an automatic.
Truth: Actually, that one is probably true.

Did You Know?

→ It is often said that people resemble their dogs. What is less well known is that many of these same people drive cars that also resemble their dogs. This is because it is difficult for people who look like dogs to find regular employment.

Signs You Should Probably Hold Off Buying That Used Car You Have Your Eye On

A tow bar.

Indicates car may have been used to tow heavy objects like boats, houses, houseboats or boat houses.

That fresh, ocean smell inside.

Could just be the result of previous owner being a fun-loving beach dweller, but could also indicate the vehicle has spent some time submerged in the ocean. Also, the descriptive phrase, "fun-loving" is not

	what you're looking for in a previous owner.
An odometer reading of 13 miles on that cute 1948 De Soto.	Possibly, car has only been driven 13 miles. More likely, odometer has rolled over, and actual mileage is 1,000,013 miles.
Important body parts like fenders, doors, the hood or the trunk is a different color than the rest of the car.	Could be bold design statement. Probably not.
Blood stains in the trunk.	Shouldn't affect the mechanical viability of the car, but could be difficult to explain to per-spective in-laws.

Did You Know?

According to page 32 of the *2003 California Driver's Handbook,* one of the lesser-known rules which "you must know" is:

→ "Do not shoot firearms at traffic signs."

Did You Know?

According to the State of California DMV in their "Potentially Unsafe Driver" pamphlet, the following behav-iors may indicate that a driver is potentially unsafe. (In this helpful pamphlet which we quote *verbatim,* the DMV requests that you check off boxes next to behaviors you have observed in a potentially unsafe driver.)

Driving Behavior

- ☐ "Stops for no reason."
- ☐ "Is confused by traffic."
- ☐ "Turns in front of oncoming cars."
- ☐ "Applies brake and gas pedals at the same time."
- ☐ "Drives on sidewalk."
- ☐ "Falls asleep while driving."
- ☐ "Drives on wrong side of the road."
- ☐ "Does not see or react to other cars, pedestrians, etc."

The California DMV encourages citizens to report drivers who exhibit any of these behaviors to them, so the DMV can "review his or her driving qualifications." We support the DMV on this, except possibly in the case of "Drives on sidewalk," which may, in some circumstances, be a resourceful alternative to clogged traffic arteries. (See Chapter on "Underutilized Lanes.")

Testimonials

We have received numerous testimonials from grateful readers of *The Bad Driver's Handbook*. Luckily we received these flattering messages before the book was published so that they could be included in it. (We actually received most of the letters because of a mix-up due to very similar P.O. Box numbers we share with a pharmaceutical company. But we still appreciate the support.) Here are a few, chosen at random:

"Before I read *The Bad Driver's Handbook* I thought I was alone. I was ashamed of my bad driving habits. Now I know there are so many others just like me. With the new techniques I've picked up I am now a more reckless, aggressive and dangerous driver than ever! I've lost 40 lbs., and no longer suffer from chronic back pain, although I have experienced some minor whiplash recently. It's like I'm starting a new life from the beginning. Thanks, *Bad Driver's Handbook!*"

—Karen S., Alamogordo, New Mexico

"Thanks, Cialis. I still can't convince women to sleep with me, but I now know, should the opportunity arise, I'll be ready!"

—Chris W., Charlotte, North Carolina

"Dear Cialis, I'm an aspiring serial rapist, but I've always been hesitant due to a lack of confidence and low self esteem. Your product has changed my life!"

—Ted M., Eugene, Oregon

Bad Driver's Famous Last Words

Severe tire damage, my a**!

Watch this!

Why don't you get out of your car, come over here and tell me that to my face?

Don't worry. There are never any cops around here.

Are you kidding me? This thing was *built* for off-roading!

Summary

Just as you imagined that this chapter was a coherent collection of related concepts, feel free to imagine this summary concludes it in a way that is concise and memorable.

CHAPTER 42

Final Exam

Note: You may not use *The Bad Driver's Handbook* as a reference source while taking this test, unless nobody is watching you.

1. Reading this book has made me:
A) a better person.
B) appreciate the small things in life.
C) more understanding of people with different viewpoints than myself.
D) are we talking about the same book?

2. Select the pair that best expresses a relationship similar to that expressed in the original pair.
STOP SIGN: BAD DRIVER:
A) Quantum Mechanics: Kangaroo
B) Superfluous: Pedestrian
C) Cogitation: Big, Useless Word

3. Your last moving violation was given to you because:
A) They have quotas. It was the end of the month.
B) Entrapment.
C) "The Man" is trying to keep you down.

4. The DMV is:
A) evil.
B) sadistic and evil.
C) really very evil and bad.

Math Section

1. Let x be the positive integer for the speed limit, and y be the positive integer for your speed. It is safe to assume that:

A) y is greater than the quantity of x.
B) y is much greater than the quantity of x.
C) y is completely independent of the quantity of x
D) y doesn't give a rat's ass what the quantity of x is.

Essay Questions

Answer *all three* of the following questions:

1. Is being a pedestrian a biological dysfunction or a deviant lifestyle choice?

2. Describe in detail why the DMV is an evil, administrative embodiment of Lucifer, using specific examples to support your argument.

3. In what ways has the DMV come to represent all that is unjust, treasonous, decadent and wrong with the world today?

If You Like *The Bad Driver's Handbook*, You'll Love *The Dog Ate My Resumé*

THE DOG ATE MY RESUMÉ

SURVIVAL TIPS FOR LIFE AFTER COLLEGE

LEARN HOW TO:
Plunder Resources at Your University!
• Develop a Go-Getter Attitude! (Or at Least Fake One) • Be Fashionably Late for Job Interviews! • Weigh the Pros and Cons of Living at Home! (Contains No Pros) • Bring an Abrupt End to Conversations About Your Future!

Includes Survival Tips for Parents, Too!

ZACK ARNSTEIN, CLASS OF '02
LARRY ARNSTEIN, CLASS OF '67

"If the stress and disappointment of looking for a job make you want to quit, try a healthy dose of humor. Zack and Larry Arnstein's book is loaded with laugh-out-loud mock "Do's" to ease your way into the working world . . . *The Dog Ate My Resumé* is great pick-me-up reading to remind yourself that while you may be occupationally challenged at the moment, you definitely are not a bum." —*USA Today*

"Along with jug chablis, pirated cable, and a big spattering pot of lentil soup, *The Dog Ate My Resumé* is a must have for all under-employed 21-year-olds! (Or 32-year-olds, depending on how much time you wasted while trying to graduate college.) A hilarious and fast read." —Sandra Tsing Loh, author and radio commentator

Anyone who has ever graduated from college has faced the daunting question of "What am I going to do with my life?" A fortunate few know exactly what they want to do. Most of us don't have a clue.

In *The Dog Ate My Resumé: Survival Tips for Life After College*, Zack and Larry Arnstein offer comical commentary and tongue-in-cheek observations on how to:

- Plunder Resources at Your University
- Develop a Go-Getter Attitude! (Or at Least Fake One)
- Be Fashionably Late for Job Interviews
- Weigh the Pros and Cons of Living at Home! (Contains No Pros)
- Bring an Abrupt End to Conversations About Your Future

$11.95   Call 1-800-784-9553

Books Available
from Santa Monica Press

American Hydrant
by Sean Crane
176 pages $24.95

The Book of Good Habits
*Simple and Creative Ways to
Enrich Your Life*
by Dirk Mathison
224 pages $9.95

The Butt Hello
*and other ways my cats
drive me crazy*
by Ted Meyer
96 pages $9.95

Calculated Risk
*The Extraordinary Life of
Jimmy Doolittle*
by Jonna Doolittle Hoppes
360 pages $24.95

**Can a Dead Man Strike
Out?**
Mark S. Halfon
168 pages $11.95

The Dog Ate My Resumé
by Zack Arnstein and
Larry Arnstein
192 pages $11.95

Elvis Presley Passed Here
by Chris Epting
336 pages $16.95

**Exotic Travel Destinations
for Families**
by Jennifer M. Nichols
and Bill Nichols
360 pages $16.95

Footsteps in the Fog
*Alfred Hitchcock's San
Francisco*
by Jeff Kraft and
Aaron Leventhal
240 pages $24.95

**Free Stuff & Good Deals
for Folks over 50, 2nd Ed.**
by Linda Bowman
240 pages $12.95

French for Le Snob
by Yvette Reche
400 pages $16.95

**How to Find Your Family
Roots and Write Your
Family History**
by William Latham and
Cindy Higgins
288 pages $14.95

**How to Speak
Shakespeare**
by Cal Pritner and
Louis Colaianni
144 pages $16.95

**How to Win Lotteries,
Sweepstakes, and Contests
in the 21st Century, 2nd
Edition**
by Steve "America's
Sweepstakes King" Ledoux
224 pages $14.95

**Jackson Pollock:
Memories Arrested in Space**
by Martin Gray
216 pages $14.95

James Dean Died Here
*The Locations of America's Pop
Culture Landmarks*
by Chris Epting
312 pages $16.95

**The Largest U.S. Cities
Named after a Food**
by Brandt Maxwell
360 pages $16.95

Letter Writing Made Easy!
*Featuring Sample Letters for
Hundreds of Common
Occasions*
by Margaret McCarthy
224 pages $12.95

**Letter Writing Made Easy!
Volume 2**
*Featuring More Sample Letters
for Hundreds of Common
Occasions*
by Margaret McCarthy
224 pages $12.95

Life is Short. Eat Biscuits!
by Amy Jordan Smith
96 pages $9.95

Loving Through Bars
*Children with Parents in
Prison*
by Cynthia Martone
208 pages $21.95

**Marilyn Monroe Dyed
Here**
*More Locations of America's
Pop Culture Landmarks*
by Chris Epting
312 pages $16.95

Movie Star Homes
by Judy Artunian and
Mike Oldham
312 pages $16.95

Offbeat Museums
*The Collections and Curators
of America's Most Unusual
Museums*
by Saul Rubin
240 pages $19.95

A Prayer for Burma
by Kenneth Wong
216 pages $14.95

Quack!
*Tales of Medical Fraud from
the Museum of Questionable
Medical Devices*
by Bob McCoy
240 pages $19.95

Redneck Haiku
by Mary K. Witte
112 pages $9.95

**School Sense: How to
Help Your Child Succeed
in Elementary School**
by Tiffani Chin, Ph.D.
408 pages $16.95

Silent Echoes
*Discovering Early Hollywood
Through the Films of Buster
Keaton*
by John Bengtson
240 pages $24.95

Tiki Road Trip
*A Guide to Tiki Culture in
North America*
by James Teitelbaum
288 pages $16.95

Order Form 1-800-784-9553

	Quantity	Amount
American Hydrant ($24.95)	_____	_____
The Book of Good Habits ($9.95)	_____	_____
The Butt Hello . . . and Other Ways My Cats Drive Me Crazy ($9.95)	_____	_____
Calculated Risk ($24.95)	_____	_____
Can a Dead Man Strike Out? ($11.95)	_____	_____
The Dog Ate My Resumé ($11.95)	_____	_____
Elvis Presley Passed Here ($16.95)	_____	_____
Exotic Travel Destinations for Families ($16.95)	_____	_____
Footsteps in the Fog: Alfred Hitchcock's San Francisco ($24.95)	_____	_____
Free Stuff & Good Deals for Folks over 50, 2nd Ed. ($12.95)	_____	_____
French for Le Snob ($16.95)	_____	_____
How to Find Your Family Roots . . . ($14.95)	_____	_____
How to Speak Shakespeare ($16.95)	_____	_____
How to Win Lotteries, Sweepstakes, and Contests . . . ($14.95)	_____	_____
Jackson Pollock: Memories Arrested in Space ($14.95)	_____	_____
James Dean Died Here: America's Pop Culture Landmarks ($16.95)	_____	_____
The Largest U.S. Cities Named after a Food ($16.95)	_____	_____
Letter Writing Made Easy! ($12.95)	_____	_____
Letter Writing Made Easy! Volume 2 ($12.95)	_____	_____
Life is Short. Eat Biscuits! ($9.95)	_____	_____
Loving Through Bars ($21.95)	_____	_____
Marilyn Monroe Dyed Here ($16.95)	_____	_____
Movie Star Homes ($16.95)	_____	_____
Offbeat Museums ($19.95)	_____	_____
A Prayer for Burma ($14.95)	_____	_____
Quack! Tales of Medical Fraud ($19.95)	_____	_____
Redneck Haiku ($9.95)	_____	_____
School Sense ($16.95)	_____	_____
Silent Echoes: Early Hollywood Through Buster Keaton ($24.95)	_____	_____
Tiki Road Trip ($16.95)	_____	_____

	Subtotal _____
Shipping & Handling:	CA residents add 8.25% sales tax _____
1 book $3.00	Shipping and Handling (see left) _____
Each additional book is $ .50	TOTAL _____

Name ————————————————————————————

Address ————————————————————————————

City ———————————————— State ———————— Zip ——————

❏ Visa ❏ MasterCard   Card No.: ————————————————————

Exp. Date ————————————— Signature ———————————————

❏ Enclosed is my check or money order payable to:

Santa Monica Press LLC
P.O. Box 1076
Santa Monica, CA 90406
www.santamonicapress.com 1-800-784-9553